Secrets of The Yellow Brick Road

A Map for the Modern Spiritual Journey

Based on *The Wizard of Oz*

by

Jesse Stewart

SunShine Press Publications

SunShine Press Publications, Inc.
PO Box 333
Hygiene, CO 80533

Publisher's Cataloging in Publication

Stewart, Jesse
    Secrets of the yellow brick road : a map for the modern spiritual
journey / Jesse Stewart
    p. cm.
    Preassigned LCCN: 96-71662
    ISBN: 1-888604-03-4

    1. Baum, L. Frank (Lyman Frank), 1856-1919. Wizard of Oz. 2. Chil-
dren's stories, American—History and criticism. 3. Oz (Imaginary
place). 4. Self-realization. I. Title.

PS3503.A923Z78 1997   813'.4
                                       QBI96-40853

Quotations from the MGM film used with permission
from Warner Bros., a division of Time Warner Entertainment, Co.

Printed in the United States of America

5 4 3 2 1

Printed on recycled acid-free paper using soy-based ink

Dedication

This book is dedicated
to the youth of today and tomorrow,
and to all who are young at heart and
experience the longing of life.

Contents

Introduction   7

1 Dorothy's Outer World—Kansas   11

2 Dorothy's Inner World—Oz   25

3 Secrets of the Soul   37

4 Poppies   51

5 The Emerald City   63

6 Facing the Witch   71

7 Confronting the Wizard   87

8 The Guidance of the Good Witch   105

9 The Witch and the Wizard—
The Faces of Duality   117

10 Secrets of the Spirit—
From Duality to Individuality   129

11 There's No Place Like Home   145

12 The Dorothy in You   161

Introduction

The Wizard of Oz, first published in 1900 and now considered a modern American classic, celebrates its 100th anniversary with the year 2000. Author L. Frank Baum actually finished the writing of the book in 1899, but held back its publication so it would bear the date of 1900 and be considered a part of the dawning of the new century. With the book's 100th anniversary, this tale proves its power and vitality in crossing generations and spanning the globe in popularity.

What has caused *The Wizard of Oz* to have such cultural preeminence? Some may suggest it is due to the MGM film which employed the newly developed Technicolor, and has become an annual television tradition. But the story's popularity was well established before that. By the time of the film's release in 1939, the book had already sold over ten million copies and been read by an estimated eighty million people. Even the stage production, which Baum produced himself, received notable success. Opening in Chicago in 1903, then moving to Broadway for a record-breaking 293 performances, it went on to tour an unprecedented 941 U.S. cities up until 1911.

The secret of the success of *The Wizard of Oz* is in the secrets it possesses. Baum had a marvelously fertile imagination. He employed it in many entrepreneurial endeavors as he roamed the U.S. in his early days, after the family fortune went bust. He also used it to spin many tales for the young and young at heart. He felt a mission to create stories that were distinctly modern and distinctly American—a departure from the European ones with which he had been raised. And so he was open to receive inspirations that would serve modern consciousness while staying in touch with the eternal.

When it came to *The Wizard of Oz,* even to Baum himself it stood out as distinct from all his other reveries. He could scarcely get it on paper fast enough as it spilled into the chalice of his imagination. Later in his life he was quoted to have said, "It was pure inspiration. It came to me right out of the blue. I think that sometimes the Great Author has a message to get across and He has to use the instrument at hand. I happened to be that medium, and I believe the magic key was given to me to open the doors to sympathy and understanding, joy, peace and happiness." The spiritual side of Baum recognized the power of stories to communicate messages of spiritual content. *The Wizard of Oz* proves to be just that, and Baum's greatest service to such a cause.

As with any tale of this nature, its origin is in the beyond—*the Land of the Archetypes* one might say. Storytelling, which has been a part of all cultures everywhere, has traditionally been an oral one, where tales can take on new shape and emphasis with each new telling. As a result, we often have many different versions of the same tale. A storyteller is free to live in the moment and draw in inspiration freshly each time, dressing it with the characters, and serving it up as living nourishment to the audience. The written form only came with the advent of the written word, and the film medium even more recently. This is not to discredit the value of these forms of media, they each have their advantages and disadvantages. But it is to remind the reader that a story is derived from a place beyond its vehicle of communication and should not be restricted to those presentations. All this is being said to prepare the reader for the presentation in this book.

This book points to a tale that points to something else. I take my primary cue from the unabridged Baum. But I also, although with reluctance at first, have come to appreciate the MGM film as an occurrence where much of what it communicates is true to its source. Furthermore, the film, through the mysterious collaboration of varied artists, adds its own significant insights—parts that are an adjunct to Baum's telling. The film acts as an artistic extension of the original story. This being the case, I have been liberal in quoting both book and film, as well as adding my own thoughts—all the while endeavoring to stay true to the spirit of the story.

It is this same inspiration that arouses in so many an intrigue with this story, as it teases our latent wisdom, dangling secrets before us—secrets of the Yellow Brick Road. But really there are no secrets. As Goethe put it—Life is an "open secret." All we have to do is be open to hear, and take the time to look. Fairy tales are like dreams. They are riddles to be unlocked and mysteries to be explored. This is the approach this book takes. It endeavors to go with the reader in the opening of the story's deeper meaning, a journey to its source, a feast on its marrow—where the soul and spirit can find nourishment. It is not so much an analysis of the story as it is an encounter with it. It is a journey through the journey.

One hundred years have passed since Baum received his "out of the blue" inspiration. One hundred years and more will pass again as it continues as a source of inspiration. As the inscription at the beginning of the film says in reference to the story, "Time has been powerless to put its kindly philosophy out of fashion." The intent of this book is to explore that "kindly philosophy," to understand its message for our modern times, and to see how it may serve as *a map for the modern spiritual journey.*

1

Dorothy's Outer World—Kansas

A World Without Color

When we first meet Dorothy we are meeting someone who is about to begin an incredible journey. But before it starts, we should note what author L. Frank Baum takes the time to describe at the outset of her adventure. It is unusual for a fairy tale to describe the outer circumstances of the person who is about to embark on an inner journey, but in doing so it highlights the relationship between our inner and outer worlds.

To begin with, Dorothy's outer world is gray—colorless. "When Dorothy stood in the doorway and looked around, she could see nothing but the gray prairie on every side. Not a tree, nor a house broke the broad sweep of flat country that reached to the edge of the sky in all directions. The sun had baked the ploughed land into a gray mass, with little cracks running through it."

The grayness and flatness of the landscape is reflected in Dorothy's home. "Once the house had been painted, but the sun blistered the paint and the rains washed it away, and now the house was dull and gray as everything else."

Even those around Dorothy are described with the same tone. Of the sun's and wind's effect on Auntie Em, "they had taken the sparkle from her eyes and left them a sober gray; they had taken the red from her cheeks and lips, and they were gray also. She was thin and gaunt, and never smiled now." Uncle Henry "never laughed. He worked hard from morning till night and did not know what joy was. He was gray also, from his long beard to his rough boots, and he looked stern and rarely spoke." All is gray in Dorothy's outer world.

In the film version a cinematic effect is used to emphasize the grayness. Although color is used for later scenes, a particularly washed out black and white film technique is used for the Kansas scenes to make everything look especially gray. It purposely accentuates the dullness and flatness of Dorothy's outer surroundings to contrast it with what is to follow. It also implies the possibility of Dorothy becoming dull and gray herself—if something doesn't change. Will she become washed out like Auntie Em and Uncle Henry?

So far, Dorothy has maintained some color in her otherwise gray world. "When Dorothy, who was an orphan, first came to her, Aunt Em had been startled by the child's laughter, that she would scream and press her hand upon her heart whenever Dorothy's merry voice reached her ears; and she still looked at the little girl with wonder that she could find anything to laugh at." Dorothy's exuberance is largely due to her dog, Toto. "It was Toto that made Dorothy laugh, and saved her from growing as gray as her surroundings. Toto was not gray; he was a little black dog, with long silky hair and small black eyes that twinkled merrily on either side of his funny, wee nose. Toto played all day long, and Dorothy played with him, and loved him dearly."

But how long can Dorothy stay in this state of innocence? How long can she continue the life of a child, playing all the time and depending on a pet to sustain her amidst the hardening effects of the material world? How long can she live in a one-sided world without becoming one-sided herself? Will she become colorless? Will she eventually succumb to an arid existence as the others? Or is there some way for her to rise above the flatness of the cultural wasteland surrounding her? Ominously, something looms on the horizon.

"Today, however, they were not playing. Uncle Henry sat upon the doorstep and looked anxiously at the sky, which was grayer than usual. Dorothy stood in the door with Toto in her arms, and looked at the sky too. Aunt Em was washing the dishes." As the grayness grows, Uncle Henry sits watching it come and Auntie Em keeps on with the dishes. What about Dorothy, what will she do?

Dorothy the Orphan

No more details are given about Dorothy's background except that she is an orphan. The orphan, as an archetype, appears in many fairy tales and is an interesting one to consider. Orphans are without their real parents. They lack that connection. They have an unspoken question, "Who are my *real* parents?"

We are all orphans in a sense. In our spiritual nature we are orphans. Physically we all have parents—they gave us physical life. But our spiritual side just as much needs its spiritual parentage—that we may have spiritual life. The archetype of the orphan represents that part of us that silently asks the questions, "Where is my spiritual parentage? How am I going to grow spiritually? What is the power that will allow me to rise to my fullest potential?" Dorothy is that part of us that wants to know that power. At this stage Dorothy is still looking for it in those around her.

Auntie Em and Uncle Henry

In the book, Dorothy's inner journey begins almost immediately. In fact, the very first chapter is entitled, "The Cyclone," and by the third page she is on her way to Oz. But the opening scenes of the film introduce more about Dorothy's outer situation. The first shot we see of Dorothy is her returning home from school. When she arrives she goes straight to Auntie Em and Uncle Henry. She is quite upset because Toto apparently just bit the neighbor, Miss Gulch, who hit Toto over the back with a rake. And furthermore, Miss Gulch says she's going to tell the Sheriff. This obviously has Dorothy concerned. She wants Auntie Em and Uncle Henry to help her with her situation.

As Aunt and Uncle, Auntie Em and Uncle Henry are not Dorothy's real parents, but rather her guardians. They act as surrogate parents to Dorothy. The question about Dorothy's parents becomes an important one as the story unfolds. The words "parent" and "prepare" share the same Latin root. "To parent" and "to prepare" have the similar meaning, "to get ready." To parent means to prepare or get ready. I like to refer to our birth parents as our "preparents." As they *parent* us they *prepare* us for what lies ahead. And so Auntie Em and Uncle Henry are Dorothy's preparents, having done what they can to get her ready for what is to come.

Cutting the Cord

When Dorothy goes to Auntie Em and Uncle Henry for help, they are of course working and have their own problems. She is told they are too busy and to not bother them. Something is wrong with the incubator and they are concerned about losing their baby chicks. For this reason they push Dorothy away. Dorothy persists a bit but then gives up and walks away.

Auntie Em and Uncle Henry are unwilling to help Dorothy at this time. But perhaps this is for the better—perhaps they are unable. They are having a hard enough time with some newborn chicks, much less equipped to help Dorothy with her hatching soul. It is apparent the time is approaching for the cord to be cut between Dorothy and her dependencies. As well-meaning as Uncle Henry and Aunt Em may be, they are ultimately unable to be for Dorothy what she needs to be for herself. It is time for her to let go of life on the farm as she knows it and move out to a broader scope of existence.

Dorothy needs to exchange this relationship for something more universal. A connection to her *spiritual parentage* awaits in the wings. The pretense of the broken incubator is but a gentle nudging in this direction. Meeting this outer wall of resistance, Dorothy is being turned to her inner world—to awaken to her own resources. But before she does this, she still looks elsewhere for help.

The Three Farm Hands

When Dorothy is turned away by Auntie Em and Uncle Henry, she then gives the three farm hands a try. Each of the farm hands is more than willing to offer their advice. The first one she approaches is Hunk. While working away on a wagon he says, "Now look it Dorothy, you ain't using your head about Miss Gulch. Think you didn't have any brains at all!" Dorothy responds, "I have so got brains!" Hunk retorts, "Well, why don't you use 'em!...Your head ain't made of straw you know!" In the next breath he hits himself on the hand with a hammer.

Next Dorothy approaches Zeke, who's feeding the hogs. While Dorothy is doing a balancing act on the fence rail, we hear him talking tough to a hog, "Get in there before I make a dime bag out of ya!" In reference to Miss Gulch, he tells Dorothy, "Listen kid, are you going to let that old Gulch heifer try and buffalo ya? She ain't nothin' to be afraid of. Have a little courage, that's all." Dorothy responds, "I'm not afraid of her." Zeke further coaches her, "The next time she squawks, walk right up to her and spit in her eye. That's what I'd do." On her next step, Dorothy falls into one of the pig pens and Zeke has to rescue her. After carrying her out, he has to sit down and it becomes apparent he is quite frightened by the incident.

Dorothy then approaches the third farm hand, Hickory. It is not quite clear what he is doing, but with a little research I discovered that the film editors cut a part out here. Hickory is actually working on a machine to ward off cyclones. Before it got edited, he says to Dorothy, "Listen, Dorothy, don't let Hunk kid you about Miss Gulch. She's just a poor, sour-faced old maid, she ain't got no heart left. You know, you should have a little more heart yourself." Dorothy responds, "I try and have a little heart." Hickory then turns her attention, "Now look here—here's something that really has heart. This is the best invention I ever invented." Auntie Em then comes along and chastises him and sternly tells them all to get back to work. Hickory then becomes proud of heart and while striking an arrogant pose vows, "Someday they're going to erect a statue to me in this town." Like the others, he is unable to back his words with his actions.

And so Dorothy can't get any real answers from anyone. Is she being let down or is she being put on a path to finding her own answers? What is significant is that each of the farm hands puts forth a different idea. The ideas of using one's brain, being courageous and having heart are presented to Dorothy. She insists that she has all three, but what state are they in?

Homelessness

A condition of *homelessness* is also implied in the archetype of the orphan. Dorothy expresses this homelessness. She has a physical home on the farm but at the same time appears out of place and in the way of others. Is this her *real* home? The farm, or wherever we reside is at best only a temporary abode on the journey of life. The orphan asks, "Where is my real home?"

Dorothy is the part of us that longs for our true home. Dorothy needs to discover the true nature of "home." There is a restlessness about her. She does not know where she came from or where she belongs. A quest needs to take place. Dorothy has not yet done this and Auntie Em underscores it by telling her to, "Find yourself a place where you won't get into any trouble." "Find yourself a place..." hits Dorothy as a new thought and tips the scale of her awakening a bit further.

The Longing of Life

Dorothy walks off with Toto to ponder Auntie Em's words, "Find yourself a place..." One of the most powerful qualities Dorothy conveys in these opening scenes is her connection to her sense of yearning. She is experiencing a hunger. It is *the longing of life.*

The outer circumstances are applying pressure to Dorothy, while at the same time giving her little outer assistance to deal with them. She is expressing some of the frustration and lack of satisfaction we all experience in this world. But instead of becoming numb to it, she expresses her deeply felt longing in her lamenting song about somewhere over the rainbow. It is an indeterminate yearning in Dorothy at this point, unclear where it wants to take her, except—somewhere over the rainbow. Nevertheless she is becoming aware of her inner stirring and makes a real connection to it.

Something of vast importance is being pointed to in the ominous mood of the opening scenes. As we see rays of light breaking through the gray clouds, it signifies the calling from the other world—the beckoning to the other side. Dorothy is experiencing the tug of her inner world, as she struggles with the challenges of her outer one. But she is still largely engulfed in the grayness of the outer world, unconscious and unacquainted with this other side of herself.

Dorothy's yearning for somewhere over the rainbow points to the primordial passion and hunger to reconnect with the spiritual origins of life—the true source of color for our otherwise gray, mundane existence. Dorothy is giving voice to this tension between the two worlds—the split we all experience with some degree of awareness. And now the emerging circumstances are preparing to remove the veil of innocence that keeps secret the "other side" and stops Dorothy from experiencing the fullness of life.

What About Toto?

The most frequently asked question about *The Wizard of Oz* as an allegory must be, "What about Toto?" Toto is obviously Dorothy's dear pet and companion. "Toto played all day long, and Dorothy played with him, and loved him dearly." But he has been more than that for Dorothy. "It was Toto that made Dorothy laugh, and saved her from growing as gray as her surroundings." Toto has been the source of life for Dorothy in an otherwise dreary world—keeping her alive inside. Obviously much of her sense of self is derived from Toto. But how long can he be for Dorothy what she needs to be for herself? Something needs to change.

A crisis is breaking and a shift beginning in Dorothy's life. She has a problem on her hands and ironically Toto is the one who started it. It is because he chased Miss Gulch's cat through her garden, then bit her when she hit him with a rake, that Dorothy's otherwise unperturbed existence is becoming troubled. It would be unfair to put full blame on Toto for the unfolding chaos. He is simply triggering a process that is looking for a place to happen. In this sense he is actually acting as an extension of Dorothy and doing her a service—despite the difficulty he is creating.

Almira Gulch

Almira Gulch is a wealthy and snooty old maid. She is the rich witch of the county and seems to savor the part. She already has lots, but wants more. She has an appetite for power that knows no satisfaction, even to the point of wanting to destroy a little girl's dear pet. Typical of a power tripper, when Toto takes a nip at her, she takes the opportunity to wield her weight. Without wasting a moment she shows up at the farm with Sheriff's papers in one hand, and a basket in the other. She has come to take Toto away to be destroyed.

Dorothy is shocked by what is happening, "Destroyed? Toto? Oh, you can't...you mustn't. Auntie Em, Uncle Henry, you won't let her, will you?" Uncle Henry stammers, "Of course we won't...will we Em?" Dorothy looks at Auntie Em who says nothing. Auntie Em and Uncle Henry just stand there getting grayer by the minute. There is nothing either of them can do to stop Miss Gulch or to help Dorothy. Dorothy becomes angry and tries to stop Miss Gulch herself, "Oh no, I won't let you take him. You go away...I'll bite you myself! You wicked old witch!" But her efforts to resist Miss Gulch and pleas to Auntie Em and Uncle Henry are to no avail. Almira Gulch puts Toto in her basket and takes him away on her bicycle.

But then the unexpected happens—serendipity at work. Toto escapes from the basket and runs back to Dorothy, "Toto, darling! Oh I got you back! You came back! Oh, I'm so glad." Then she realizes, "Oh, they'll be coming back for you in a minute," and comes to the monumental conclusion, "We've got to get away!"

Dorothy then makes the unprecedented and weighty decision to leave her home. With Toto at her side, she takes her first steps out into the greater world.

Professor Marvel

As Dorothy and Toto set out into the unknown, they encounter a whimsical old gentleman. He is a traveling medicine show type, who goes by the name of *Professor Marvel*. After a bit of small talk Dorothy asks if she can travel with him to the far lands his signs advertise about. With all the airs of a polished charlatan, he insists he must consult his crystal ball before doing anything. Being the talented impostor that he is, he dons an impressive turban, lights some candles, and boasts of his connection to the ancient Egyptian mysteries of Isis and Osiris. He then asks her to close her eyes, and while telling her he's reaching out into "the infinite," reaches into her basket for clues as to who she is.

Even though he's a fraud and a *not-so-wonderful wizard*, Professor Marvel is still basically a kind person. After getting an idea as to who Dorothy is, (from a picture he found in her basket), he pretends that he sees Auntie Em in the crystal ball—stricken with grief. She is apparently distraught over the disappearance of Dorothy and clutching her heart. Dorothy is moved by this supposed revelation and utters the words, "Oh, I've got to go home right away!" Professor Marvel says, "I thought you were going along with me?" But no, Dorothy is now in an urgent mode to get back home, and leaves immediately with Toto. Professor Marvel, noticing a storm working up, says to himself, "Poor little kid. I hope she gets home alright."

The Ripping Twister

As Dorothy heads back to the farm something else is heading that way also. Out of the darkening gray blows a storm to change the face of the outer landscape as well as Dorothy's inner one. It is a cyclone.

Sometimes storms can be greatest gifts in how they awaken us from our spiritual slumber, especially if we have overslept in innocence. The cyclone has come to tear the embryonic veil of Dorothy's yet unshed naivete and open the way to her inner world—it is a ripping twister. Dorothy is ready for an awakening and the wind has come to introduce her to the secrets of her inner world.

The Bridge to the Other Side:
Dorothy Takes Oz by Storm

When Dorothy arrives back at the farm she can't find anyone else. They have all retreated to the safety of the storm shelter. Dorothy is left alone with the winds of change. This is where the book picks up the plot, "A strange thing then happened. The house whirled around two or three times and rose slowly through the air. Dorothy felt as if she were going up in a balloon."

At this point Dorothy doesn't know what is happening to her—or what is *endeavoring* to happen to her. She no doubt would have chosen different circumstances for herself. But the circumstances have determined for her that she be thrown into the spiraling chaos of the storm. "As the hours passed and nothing terrible happened, she stopped worrying and resolved to wait calmly and see what the future would bring." Dorothy decides to just flow with it.

Dorothy is being carried over to the other side—the "inner world." Entering the inner realm is portrayed in many ways in many stories, just as it can take place in real life in various ways. In some stories it is depicted as the crossing of a bridge—spanning a river or chasm deep and wide. In other stories it is a wardrobe or a tunnel that is passed through. Passages such as these carry with them a mood of anticipation, as with the pulling away of veils. In this story it is a flying house, in the funnel of the tornado that indicates the move to the other side. Dorothy takes Oz by storm.

2

Dorothy's Inner World—Oz

A World of Color

After the intensity of the transition from the outer realm to the inner one is over, all becomes still. "Dorothy sat up and noticed that the house was not moving; nor was it dark, for the bright sunshine came in at the window, flooding the little room. She sprang from her bed and with Toto at her heels ran and opened the door. The little girl gave a cry of amazement and looked about her, her eyes growing bigger and bigger at the wonderful sights she saw." The view through Dorothy's doorway is now quite different than before. Baum goes on in detail describing this curious world, as Dorothy crosses the threshold into the Land of Oz.

In the film, with the help of the newly developed Technicolor, the scene changes from black and white to rich and radiant color. This effect must have been almost as breathtaking for those experiencing a color film for the first time, as it was for Dorothy to get her first glimpse of the Land of Oz. The contrasting of color to black and white is much more than a cinematic gimmick. It points to the true source of color—the inner world, the world beyond this one. This is what has been missing in the gray of Dorothy's outer life—a connection to her inner world.

Lost in the Land of Oz

Dorothy doesn't know where she is—she is totally and utterly lost. Where she is, in her inner realm, is where the events of her outer realm have taken her. The chaotic outer circumstances, and her response to them have broken new ground in Dorothy's consciousness, and placed her in an unfamiliar inner space. She is illustrating another motif of the archetypal journey—*being lost.*

After a short survey of the foreign surroundings, Dorothy utters those oft-quoted words, "Toto, I have a feeling we're not in Kansas anymore." Then she muses, "We must be over the rainbow." She is in fact, and this is Munchkinland.

Munchkins

What is Munchkinland and what are Munchkins? The occupants of the area slowly begin to approach Dorothy. "While she stood looking eagerly at the strange and beautiful sights, she noticed coming towards her a group of the queerest people she had ever seen. They were not as big as the grown folk she had always been used to." She is encountering the "little folk" or the *elemental beings* of the invisible realm.

The Munchkins are at first wary of Dorothy, and reluctant to reveal themselves. "When these people drew near the house where Dorothy was standing in the doorway they paused and whispered among themselves, as if afraid to come farther." Their caution is justified. We learn that they have been held captive in their own land by an oppressive force—the Wicked Witch of the East. Before they will get too close they need assurance that it is okay. And so the Munchkins summon the Good Witch.

The Good Witch

Out of the blue, slowly coming into view, floats the Good Witch. Upon her arrival Dorothy is asked, "Are you a good witch or a bad witch?" Dorothy replies in bewilderment, "Who me? Why—I'm not a witch at all. I'm Dorothy Gale from Kansas." To the tittering of Munchkins she states, "Witches are old and ugly." The Good Witch too is amused by this and responds that, despite her beauty, she is a witch and that "only bad witches are ugly."

The Good Witch of the book makes her entrance a little differently. "The little old woman walked up to Dorothy, made a low bow, and said in a sweet voice, 'You are welcome most noble Sorceress to the land of the Munchkins. We are so grateful to you for having killed the Wicked Witch of the East, and for setting our people free from bondage.' Dorothy listened to this speech with wonder. What could the little woman possibly mean by calling her a sorceress, and saying she had killed the Wicked Witch of the East?" Dorothy replies, "'You are very kind; but there must be some mistake. I have not killed anything.' 'Your house did anyway,' replied the little old woman with a laugh, 'and that is the same thing. See!' Dorothy looked, and gave a little cry of fright. There, indeed, just under the corner of the great beam the house rested on, two feet were sticking out, shod in silver shoes with pointed toes. 'Oh, dear! Oh, dear!' cried Dorothy, clasping her hands together in dismay. 'The house must have fallen on her. Whatever shall we do?' 'There is nothing to be done,' said the little woman calmly. 'But who was she?' asked Dorothy. 'She was the Wicked Witch of the East, as I said,' answered the little woman. 'She has held all the Munchkins in bondage for many years, making them slave to her night and day. Now they are all set free, and are grateful to you for the favor.'"

The Wicked Witch of the East

Fanfare and merriment breaks out in Munchkinland as news spreads that the Wicked Witch has been crushed in the ditch. Bells ring and voices sing, resounding how the Wicked Witch of the East at last is dead.

What does the Wicked Witch of the East represent in this tale? If fairy tales are psychological portraits, and if *The Wizard of Oz* is true to this fashion, then all of what we are being introduced to in the Land of Oz are facets of Dorothy's inner life. The Wicked Witch of the East was something of Dorothy—something that was oppressing other parts. But Dorothy has brought an end to this, setting Munchkinland free.

What has occurred in Dorothy's inner land is a reflection of something that took place in her outer world. Our outer actions and inner state of being are inseparable. They are inextricably connected to each other and continually affecting each other. The death of the Wicked Witch of the East is an echo of something in Dorothy's outer life.

Dorothy's Declaration of Independence

Besides all the outer action in the opening episodes, something significant took place—between the lines. Something took place in Dorothy. She responded to the difficult circumstances surrounding her with action and initiative.

When Miss Gulch arrived to take Toto away, Dorothy turned to the others for help. But when no one came to her rescue, she then took matters into her own hands, finding her voice and standing up to Miss Gulch. But Miss Gulch had the weight of the law with her and left with Toto. Toto escaped however and came back to Dorothy. With this Dorothy knew she had to make a move of her own and decided to run away. This action was a clear step out from under the roof and parentage of Auntie Em and Uncle Henry. This signaled a breaking free from her dependency on them. Dorothy made a personal "declaration of independence."

Just as the three farm hands advised Dorothy, she used her own brain, heart and courage. It took thinking to know she needed to run away. It took heart to want to return home. And courage to do both. She took initiative which initiated her capacities of thinking, feeling and will. Instead of being dependent on others for these things she exercised her own powers. She shifted from a dependency on others to a dependency on herself.

The death of the Wicked Witch of the East is symbolic of the end of Dorothy's dependency—the cutting of the cord. Had she not brought an end to this, crushing it in the ditch as with the landing of her house, it would have gone on as an oppressive factor in her life. It would have been a restrictive element to her growth, preventing her from having an inner life of her own. But Dorothy's *initiative* was a declaration of independence, breaking her free from this outgrown aspect. Her decisions and actions in the outer world affected her inner world in this way. The Munchkins now consider her their national heroine and the Mayor of Munchkinland fittingly proclaims it "a day of independence."

Dorothy's New Shoes

The death of the Witch is more than an end, it is also a new beginning. The death of the Witch is better termed "a transformation." The power the Witch once had is transformed and transferred to Dorothy. This is seen symbolically in the transfer of the magic slippers from the Wicked Witch's feet to Dorothy's. Dorothy is now endowed with the Witch's power. This once oppressive part now exists in a new way for her. Rather than being imprisoned by it, she is empowered by it.

In the film the shoes suddenly and surprisingly appear on Dorothy's feet. In the book, she actually decides to take the shoes for herself, to help her on her journey. "'I wonder if they will fit me. They would be just the thing to take a long walk in, for they could not wear out.' She took off her old leather shoes and tried on the silver ones, which fitted her as well as if they had been made for her."

The shoes are silver in the book. Hollywood however used its artistic license to make them red. Being such a focal point of the story, it was deemed best not to put silver shoes on the silver screen, when wanting to make the most of the new color technology. Thus the *ruby slippers* were born.

The Wicked Witch of the West

Nothing like rain on a parade. Just as the jubilation over Dorothy's accomplishment is reaching fever pitch, out of an explosion of fire and smoke emerges another unsightly character. Dorothy turns to the Good Witch in alarm. The Good Witch explains, "This is the Wicked Witch of the West. And she's worse than the other one was." In the book the Good Witch merely introduces Dorothy to the fact that there is another Wicked Witch, but in the film she shows up with a vengeance to find out, "Who killed my sister?" Pointing her crooked finger at Dorothy she asks accusatively, "Was it you?" Dorothy responds, "No, no! It was an accident."

Next, the Wicked Witch's attention turns to the magic slippers. Now that Dorothy has been empowered with them, this other Wicked Witch wants to disempower her, so she can have the upper hand in Oz. Dorothy's naivete about the nature of the slippers is revealed in her ambivalence toward them. But the Good Witch warns her to keep tight in the shoes for their magic is very powerful, then dismisses the Wicked Witch from Munchkinland. Exuding some more nastiness, the Wicked Witch threatens Dorothy, "I'll get you my pretty, and your little dog too!" With a burst of laughter, she whirls around and vanishes in a clap of thunder and a cloud of sulfurous gas.

Dorothy's Dilemma

Dorothy is left quite frightened by this encounter. She doesn't like it in this place so much anymore. In the book she sobs with the loneliness she feels in these unfamiliar surroundings. The Munchkins weep with her. Dorothy decides she wants to go back to Kansas.

This is an interesting turn. When Dorothy was in Kansas she was longing for somewhere over the rainbow. Now that she's here she wants to leave. What's wrong with Dorothy, can't she make up her mind? Is the grass always greener on the other side? Or is this dilemma pointing to something of greater significance?

Dorothy is illustrating *the tension between the two worlds*. She is in a dilemma, caught in a quandary—betwixt and between. In Kansas, Dorothy was split between running away with Professor Marvel to see the world and returning to the farm. This is now reflected in her inner world as being caught between wanting to be over the rainbow and being back on the farm. This dilemma is also archetypal.

Dorothy is expressing what we all experience in our lives, something basic to existence—the tension between two options. Dorothy's dilemma is not just about being on the farm or not being on the farm, or about being over the rainbow or not being over the rainbow. It is about resolving the tension of the two by finding where the dilemma leads.

Dorothy's dilemma, as a dilemma will do, is presenting her with an opportunity to find a new perspective and to get a new vision. It is challenging her to go further in exploring where this universal yearning she has connected with will take her. As the lost and homeless orphan, it is raising for her the question "Where is home?"

At this point for Dorothy, *being home* means being back on the farm with Auntie Em and Uncle Henry—it even sounds homey. But if we remember how things were when she was there, we will recall how gray it was, and an illusion for Dorothy to think that's where her ultimate destination lies. But Dorothy feels threatened in these new surroundings and is looking for something familiar that will give her hope and comfort. Of course it is only natural for her to think of something she knows. We all at times are given to seeking security in things that have given it to us in the past, rather than in something of an uncertain future. But the tension of Dorothy's dilemma is driving her forward to discover something new in her life.

Dorothy's Question

Dorothy is determined to get back to Kansas but realizes she can't go back the way she came. This new circumstance forces Dorothy to ask the question—*How do I get home?* Dorothy's dilemma has placed before her the ultimate quest and question of existence—*Where is home and how do I get there?*

The Yellow Brick Road

Even though Dorothy is determined to return to Kansas, she is faced with a real problem. The Land of Oz is surrounded by an impassable desert. There is no immediate solution at hand. The Good Witch does a little divination with her magic wand and her hat, turning the hat into a slate. It has a message on it, written in big, white chalk letters saying, "LET DOROTHY GO TO THE CITY OF EMERALDS." This serves as an intermediate solution. The Good Witch suggests that the Wizard of Oz will help her.

When Dorothy asks, "How do I start for the Emerald City?" the Good Witch advises, "It's always best to start at the beginning." The Good Witch then finalizes the directions with, "All you do is follow the Yellow Brick Road," pointing at it with her wand. When told to, "Follow the Yellow Brick Road," Dorothy plies for more information with, "But what happens if..." The Good Witch interrupts with, "Just follow the Yellow Brick Road," then disappears. No more clues are to be given Dorothy for now. This *wise one* obviously sees things from a higher vantage point and knows the best guidance to give Dorothy at this time. In her wisdom she knows more information would only confuse Dorothy. Dorothy just needs to get going. And so, Dorothy starts her journey with little more information than, "Just follow the Yellow Brick Road." The answer to her questions and more will come on the journey.

Choosing a Path

In front of Dorothy lies a yellow brick road. But it is not the only road possible to take. There are other roads she could choose. But the Good Witch was specific it is, "the Yellow Brick Road," Dorothy is to follow. Having other roads to choose from indicates how Dorothy has a choice in the matter. Without choice there would be no freedom. But Dorothy is willing to follow the guidance of the Good Witch and without hesitation sets foot on the beginning point of the Yellow Brick Road.

This raises another question. What does it mean to, "Follow the Yellow Brick Road?" What marks the modern spiritual journey? What is the essence of what some call "the golden path," and what sets it apart from other paths? Clues to this too shall unfold as Dorothy follows the Yellow Brick Road.

The Spiral of Chaos and Creativity

The route home for Dorothy starts as a road spiraling out before her. This outward spiraling is in contrast to the inward spiraling cyclone that brought her into her inner realm to begin with.

The spiral has been considered by many cultures throughout history as a sacred symbol. Why has it been regarded as such? The spiral is more than a symbol. The people of ancient times perceived its presence as a dynamic force in all of nature. Nothing on earth is untouched by the spiraling set in motion by our spinning planet, in our spiraling galaxy.

Pine cones and seashells are clear reflections of this force. Water spirals down the drain as an indication of this action. From seed to bloom a plant's journey toward the light is a spiraling one, as evident in its stem. In our anatomy the signature of the spiral is seen in the dramatic vortex swirl at the crown of our head, to the subtle spiral gesture in our bones.

But the spiral is also associated with chaos, as seen in the tornado. It stirs things up, even causing death and destruction. But what from one perspective is viewed as destructive and chaotic is actually the other side of creativity. A cyclone is a destructive force but not necessarily a bad one. The wind is a part of nature's ways and destruction an integral part of the creative process. As D. H. Lawrence said, "The breath of life is in the sharp winds of change, mingled with the breath of destruction." It sometimes takes something with the intensity of a storm to clear the way so something new can be born.

The figurative twisters in our lives have the potential to bring out our best, as they present challenge and opportunity for change.

Both chaos and creativity are represented by the spiral. It all depends on our perspective. And the perspective we choose will determine how we respond to the potential when it presents itself to us. Will we use the creative possibilities inherent in chaos? Or will we be overrun by what we construe as threatening? Will Dorothy take her chaotic situation and use it as something with creative potential, or will she stay lost in her inner space, remaining naive to the power at her feet? Dorothy faces choices as she steps out on the Yellow Brick Road.

The Spiral of Chaos and Creativity

3

Secrets of the Soul

As Dorothy takes her first steps on the road winding out before her, she is heralded by a merry Munchkin melody, echoing the Good Witch's words, "Follow the Yellow Brick Road." In the book, before setting out, she takes time to prepare herself for the journey. When ready, she enthusiastically begins her quest for the Emerald City. Dorothy doesn't know it, but she is going to have some interesting encounters, including with three significant, if not colorful characters.

Dorothy Meets the Scarecrow

After Dorothy has gone a little way, she comes to a cornfield with a scarecrow high on a pole. The Scarecrow speaks to her, which is quite a surprise because she's not used to talking scarecrows back in Kansas. "How do you do?" "I'm pretty well, thank you," replies Dorothy politely, "How do you do?" "I'm not feeling well," says the Scarecrow with a smile, "for it is very tedious being perched up here night and day to scare away crows." "Can't you get down?" asks Dorothy. "No, for this pole is stuck up my back." Dorothy helps the Scarecrow down and we soon hear his story.

The Scarecrow claims to not have a brain. Apparently the farmer who made him gave him eyes, ears and a mouth, and everything else to be a Scarecrow, but didn't give him a brain. What makes things worse is that he can't even scare away the crows. He laments how they come from miles around just to eat in his field and laugh in his face. He attributes all of this to the fact that he hasn't got a brain.

The Scarecrow certainly is not lacking in resolve. He really wants a brain. An old crow once told him, "If you only had brains in your head you would be as good a man as any. Brains are the only thing worth having in this world." Ever since then he's been hanging on the post just thinking about having a brain.

Dorothy explains to the Scarecrow her situation, and how she is on her way to the Emerald City to see if the Wizard of Oz will help her get back home. The Scarecrow asks, "Do you think if I went with you, this Wizard would give me some brains?" Dorothy responds, "I couldn't say. But even if he didn't, you'd be no worse off than you are now." The Scarecrow sees the reason in this and so joins Dorothy on her journey down the Yellow Brick Road.

Dorothy Meets the Tin Man

While making their way, Dorothy and the Scarecrow happen upon another character. "One of the big trees had been partly chopped through, and standing beside it, with an uplifted axe in his hands was a man made entirely of tin. His head and arms and legs were jointed upon his body, but he stood perfectly motionless, as if he could not stir at all." With his barely audible groans he directs them to the oil can. After they oil his joints and he is able to move again, he tells how he was caught in the rain and completely rusted shut while out chopping wood. He thanks them for saving his life and asks, "How did you happen to be here?" Dorothy tells him, "We are on our way to the Emerald City, to see the great Oz. I want him to send me back to Kansas; and the Scarecrow wants him to put a few brains into his head."

The Tin Man then shares his own predicament. In the book version he tells a lengthy tale about his love for a Munchkin maiden, and a spell the Wicked Witch of the East put on him, causing him to injure himself. We learn how, while undergoing repairs, the tinsmith left out a heart. A knock to his chest gives a testimony to his hollowness—a resounding echo of emptiness.

The Tin Man then asks about coming along to the Emerald City. "Do you suppose Oz could give me a heart?" he asks. "Why, I guess so," Dorothy answers. "It would be as easy as to give the Scarecrow brains." So it is settled. The Tin Man joins them and off they merrily go down the Yellow Brick Road.

Dorothy Meets the Lion

As they continue, the journey takes them into an even denser forest. Slowing the pace they edge their way forward in the darkness. Dorothy then asks, "Do you suppose we'll meet any wild animals?" The Tin Man responds, "We might." followed by a fretful, "Lions and tigers and bears, oh my!" Suddenly comes a terrible roar, and bounding out before Dorothy and her newfound friends leaps a lion, swiping at everyone in sight.

"Little Toto, now that he had an enemy to face, ran barking towards the Lion. Dorothy, fearing Toto would be killed, and heedless of danger, rushed forward and slapped the Lion upon his nose as hard as she could, while she cried out: 'Don't you dare bite Toto! You ought to be ashamed of yourself, a big beast like you, to bite a poor little dog!'" We then find out what the Lion is really like when Dorothy says to him, "You are nothing but a big coward." The Lion agrees through his whimpers, "I know it."

It turns out the Lion is rather a poor representative of the King of the Beasts. He is a *cowardly lion*. He confesses he can't even count sheep to help him sleep, because he's *afraid* of sheep. He is lacking courage. The others take pity on him and each share their own plights as well as their hopes that the Wizard will give them what they are missing. "Do you think Oz could give me courage?" asks the Lion. All of them agree that it is worth a try and welcome him to join them. So off they all go resolutely down the Yellow Brick Road.

The Soul Question

Dorothy's journey along the Yellow Brick Road with her newfound companions could be referred to as a *psychological* journey. The word "psychological" is derived from the Greek word *psyche*, from which we get the word *soul*. This story could be considered as a journey into Dorothy's soul, or a *soul journey*. However, the use of the word "soul" may raise questions. Some may ask—Does the body have a soul? The answer could be given—It is the soul that has a body. But what exactly is meant by soul? How does one define soul? Can we know how the soul works? What is *the secret life of the soul?*

To look at these questions, let us leave the Yellow Brick Road for a moment and consider the physical body as a source of information about the soul. We may be missing the most obvious if we overlook our physical nature as an expression of our soul nature.

The Physical Body as a Reflection of the Soul

The soul, which in a certain sense is invisible to our sight, is in fact made visible through the physical body. Our soul nature expresses itself through our physical nature. This is not simply referring to body language, although that is part of it, but rather that the very design of the physical body reveals much about the soul.

The physical body is not only adapted to the outer world it lives in, but has evolved in a way that also expresses something of the inner world. It is designed in such a way that the soul can live in and through it.

Consider how the physical body is made up of three regions—the top or head region, the middle or chest region and then the third region which includes the digestive and reproductive area, and the limbs. In the top is the brain—which is usually associated with *thinking.* In the middle is the heart—which is usually associated with *feeling.* And in the third region we have organs and limbs, which are *doing* parts, or are associated with the *will.*

But the ability to have thoughts, feelings and a will takes more than just parts of our physical body. The three physical areas are there for the three soul capacities—thinking, feeling and will—to function in the physical world. The physical body is a vehicle for the soul. The body is an outward expression of the soul.

Back to the story. It is interesting how each of the three characters has an appearance that is similar to a part of the physical body. The Scarecrow, stuck up on a pole, looks a bit like a brain on a backbone. He is mainly head—the rest just stuffing. And he is so top-heavy he is constantly receiving assistance to stand up. With the Tin Man, it is the chest area that dominates—being big and barreled. The Lion has powerful large limbs and a long waving tail.

The Scarecrow says he can't think and that he wants a *brain*. The Scarecrow represents the thinking capacity of Dorothy's soul. The Tin Man says he lacks feelings and wants a *heart*. The Tin Man represents the feeling capacity of Dorothy's soul. The Lion says he is a coward and wants *courage*. We sometimes refer to courage as guts, indicating how the metabolic region of the physical body along with the limbs is connected with the courage or will part of the soul. The Lion represents the will capacity of Dorothy's soul. The three characters together make up the three parts of the soul—thinking, feeling and will or what could be called *the threefold soul.*

In Kansas, Dorothy was told by the three farm hands to use these three capacities in herself—not that the farm hands were good examples of these abilities. But it pointed her in the direction of getting in touch with these parts of herself. We saw these capacities come into play when she took initiative in Kansas. Now she is making direct contact with them. The personalities of the three farm hands have reemerged as the Scarecrow, Tin Man and Lion in this dreamscape. They are personifying Dorothy's newly activated thinking, feeling and will.

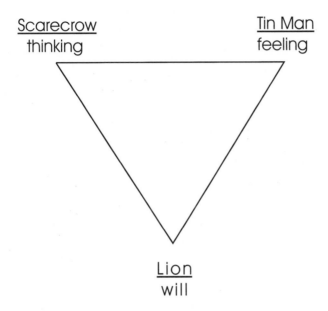

Scarecrow
thinking

Tin Man
feeling

Lion
will

The Threefold Soul

The Scarecrow Personifying
the Thinking Part of the Soul

Let us take another look at Dorothy's three encounters as *soul* encounters. Dorothy's first soul encounter is with the Scarecrow. The Scarecrow illustrates yet to be integrated thinking. He is ungrounded—being both literally and figuratively up in the air. Despite his claim to have no brain, he is well able to converse with Dorothy. But it is evident there is a problem with the Scarecrow's thinking when Dorothy asks for directions and he has trouble making up his mind. This is a rich picture of stuck thinking. It doesn't know what direction to move. Dorothy encounters the Scarecrow at an intersection in the road—a point of decision, and he is unable to help her decide. He is able to give advice, but overall is unable to offer anything of real substance at this juncture.

After Dorothy helps him off the post the Scarecrow sits down on the curb and tells her how he thinks he is a failure. He thinks he can't think. A scarecrow stuffed with straw is an interesting metaphor for thinking. Straw is dead matter. His problem is dead thinking and is just in need of something to enliven it. He admits to it being "tedious" just hanging around with a pole up his back. But is it a brain that he is missing or an opportunity to use it? His problem is that he is by himself, not yet integrated with the others. By connecting with the other parts he would be able to share his thoughts with them and receive the enlivening they would provide. And so Dorothy frees him from his isolated existence and gives him hope of fulfilling his dream to be able to think. In doing so she embraces her thinking.

Things soon start to happen for Dorothy's thinking capacity as they head out on the Yellow Brick Road. An example of *newly enlivened thinking* is seen in the enchanted apple orchard. When faced with the trees' reluctance to give up their fruit, the Scarecrow whispers to Dorothy, "I'll show you how to get apples." The Scarecrow cleverly uses a little reverse psychology, picking up an apple off the ground and throwing it at the trees, who in turn retaliate by throwing back bushels of apples. That's using her head.

The Tin Man Personifying
the Feeling Part of the Soul

When Dorothy discovers her feelings, the Tin Man, he is entirely seized up. Nothing moves. He lacks "e-motion." After Dorothy oils him we hear a great sigh as he utters, "I can talk again!" What a relief to be heard again! We can only imagine his joy—that is if he had a heart.

As the Tin Man tells his story he begins to dance. It starts off a little rusty, but after a bit he works up some *emotional steam.* He tells his sad story of how he has no heart. We see his sorrow. We hear how *downhearted* he is with no feelings to flutter about his big chest. But is it his heart that is missing or simply an opportunity to use it? We are seeing more symptoms of an unengaged, unintegrated soul part. Dorothy decides to not pass this part by either, and offers to help him by letting him join them on their journey to the Emerald City.

As they journey together an incident arises that suggests the Tin Man perhaps is capable of feelings after all. But he simply doesn't recognize them when they occur. "Once, indeed the Tin Woodman stepped upon a beetle that was crawling along the road, and killed the poor little thing. This made the Tin Woodman very unhappy, for he was always careful not to hurt any living creature; and as he walked along he wept several tears of sorrow and regret."

The heart leaps to life when they encounter the Wicked Witch in the forest. The Witch appears on the roof of the cabin and threatens to stuff a mattress with the Scarecrow and to turn the Tin Man into a beehive. It's a heated encounter and the Scarecrow is in danger of burning up when the Witch throws a fireball at him.

The Tin Man saves the day and extinguishes the fire with his cap. He is so stirred by this he becomes even more passionate about seeing that Dorothy gets to the Emerald City telling her he will help her get to see the Wizard whether he gets a heart or not. Nothing gets us going like emotions. Emotions bring us out. They get us to "emote"—from the Latin *emovere*, meaning "to move."

On another occasion, the Tin Man and the Scarecrow have a discussion about which is better—a heart or a brain? The Tin Man tells how, "the greatest loss I had known was the loss of my heart. While I was in love I was the happiest man on earth." Then he points out the greatest virtue of having feelings, "No one can love who has not a heart." But the Scarecrow defends his desire for a brain. "'I shall ask for brains instead of a heart; for a fool would not know what to do with a heart if he had one.' Dorothy did not say anything, for she was puzzled to know which of her two friends was right."

The fact is they are both right. Both thinking and feeling are needed in order to fully function as a human being. The need for love will never be fulfilled without feelings, but without thinking to keep the emotions in balance, we may be in danger of being carried away by our heart. On the other hand, without feelings to enliven our thinking we may become dry and passionless. It's an age old challenge to find the right balance between the head and the heart—thinking and feeling. But once the right balance is struck then the *will* can find its course of action.

The Lion Personifying the Will Part of the Soul

The inner landscape changes as Dorothy approaches the domain of the will. "The road was still paved with yellow bricks, but these were much covered by dried branches and dead leaves from the trees, and the walking was not at all good. Now and then there came a deep growl from some wild animal hidden among the trees. These sounds made the little girl's heart beat fast, for she did not know what made them." Dorothy comments, "Oh I don't like this forest! It's dark and creepy!" The Scarecrow responds, "I don't know, but I think it'll get darker before it gets lighter."

This "dark and creepy" place is a part of Dorothy with which she is not too familiar, and even less comfortable. It symbolizes the deepest, darkest, least conscious part of her soul. The mysterious things heard and the unevenness of the road give testimony to how inner work can get difficult as we go deeper into the unexplored parts of ourselves. But with her thoughts and feelings as companions, Dorothy treads forth into the jungle of her soul, where she meets the Lion—her will.

One doesn't hear the will spoken of as often as thinking or feeling. Probably because it is the most misunderstood, if not mysterious aspect of the soul. The will is the deepest part of the soul—deeper than our thoughts and feelings. It is the basis of our soul's posture, the bedrock of our soul's intention. The word "intention" derives from the Latin *intendere* meaning to "stretch at." Our will is what we are stretching at, or what we are aiming for. It is where our commitments lie. This part of the soul contains our deepest desires, hopes, attitudes and motivations—sometimes so deep we may not even be aware of them. But without question they effect our behavior.

When someone does something of their own will, we say they are doing it of their own *volition*. "Volition" is derived from the Latin *velle,* meaning the act of using the will—it is using one's own will or *will power.* The will is our seat of power. It gives us the power to carry out what our thoughts and feelings have conferred to do.

Why is the will being represented by a lion? The lion, in the hierarchy of animals, is called the King of the Jungle—with no predators and nothing to fear. The will should be like this in the domain of the soul. But Dorothy's will is just the opposite of this. It is a cowardly lion—afraid of everything. The Lion too is suffering from being dissociated or separated from the whole. This explains his cowardice. Without the thinking and feeling to guide it into action, the will becomes immobilized and fear is the result. Courage is only courage when it is in action. And so the Lion also wants to find the Wizard in hopes of receiving what he is lacking.

Dorothy and the Threefold Soul

The Scarecrow, Tin Man and Lion each represent an aspect of Dorothy's soul—thinking, feeling and will. But as human beings are we not more than our thoughts, feelings and actions? Are we not more than the sum of these functions? What part of us is it that experiences the life of our soul? Who stands in the middle, observing and integrating the experiences they give? What part brings together the soul capacities? Quite obviously it is Dorothy in the story. It is Dorothy who is bringing these three characters and capacities together. She stands at the center of the threefold soul.

We see what role Dorothy is playing in this gathering of parts. But what part does she represent in this dreamscape? Of what is she symbolic? In the inner world

Dorothy quite simply represents herself—or in psychological terminology "the self."

Dorothy and the Threefold Soul

The *self* is the essence of who we are. It is the part of us that recognizes itself as a being, and is aware of the fact that it has experiences. As enigmatic as it may sound, the self is the part of us that knows it is a self. The self has "self awareness."

The awakening to *self* is something that comes gradually during life's journey—an unfolding in stages. At this stage of her journey, Dorothy's self awareness is just beginning to awaken. In Kansas her personal initiative and declaration of independence showed a budding sense of self. She now wears the magic slippers as a symbol of her coming into power and consciousness.

But at the same time she is still somewhat asleep in innocence about herself—using the slippers for little more than walking. She still considers herself a little girl trying to get back to Kansas and these encounters with the others as incidental to the trip. But this perspective needs to change, and will continue to be challenged as she moves along the Yellow Brick Road. As the self, beginning to do soul work, there are miles ahead in Dorothy's awakening.

4

Poppies

The four travelers, with Toto at their heels, and great hopes that the Wizard will help them, continue their journey just as Dorothy has been instructed, following the Yellow Brick Road. But there is more for them to deal with before they reach the Emerald City. For one, they encounter "a great ditch that crossed the road and divided the forest as far as they could see on either side. It was a very wide ditch, and when they crept up to the edge and looked into it they could see it was also very deep, and there were many big, jagged rocks at the bottom. The sides were so steep that none of them could climb down, and for a moment it seemed that their journey must end." This abyss is not the only hurdle they face. They also deal with an attack by Kallidahs, which are "monstrous beasts with bodies like bears and heads like tigers."

Soul Integration

Dorothy is finding she must pass through many trials and challenges on the way to her destination. One of the purposes of the journey is to bring about a balanced integration of her soul parts—her thinking, feeling and will, or "soul integration." The journey has the potential of facilitating this purpose.

This aim can be seen by again looking at the physical body as a map or template of the soul. There it is seen how the three parts of the physical body are integrated and functioning together. The brain is in the head section, but the nervous system runs throughout the entire body. The heart is in the chest, but the circulatory system runs throughout the entire body. The limb and metabolic components, comprising the third region, also have aspects throughout the entire body. On the physical level we are already integrated and interwoven. The body shows us what we are striving for in our soul work. It is the aim of the *self* to similarly integrate the parts of the soul in a balanced manner.

The story reminds us there is everpresent opposition to this process. One example of this is seen in the forest. The Wicked Witch appears and warns the Scarecrow and Tin Man, "Stay away from her." The Witch wants to keep them apart. She knows there is power in their union that could stop her plans to disempower Dorothy and rule Oz. But opposition can also be the very thing that forges the parts together. The Scarecrow and Tin Man become even more adamant to stay with Dorothy after the Witch's threat. "I'll see you get safely to the Wizard now, whether I get a brain or not!" says the Scarecrow. The Tin Man says, "I'll see you reach the Wizard, whether I get a heart or not!" In gratitude Dorothy tells them,

"You're the best friends anybody ever had." Dorothy doesn't know just how right she is. But now that she has her three soul parts together, can she keep them together? The trials and challenges she faces are tests of her integrative work.

Poppies on the Path

The poppy field is one of the most intriguing, if not most famous parts of *The Wizard of Oz*. In the film, the group of them spot the Emerald City off in the distance and think they have as good as arrived. But first they have a poppy field to cross. It is the Wicked Witch's doing. The Witch in her determination to get the magic slippers from Dorothy has made a magic potion to put an end to them. Her spell manifests as a field of beautiful poppies, "attractive to the eye and soothing to the smell."

Baum's text reads, "Now it is well known that when there are many flowers together their odor is so powerful that anyone who breathes it falls asleep, and if the sleeper is not carried away from the scent of the flowers he sleeps on and on forever. But Dorothy did not know this, nor could she get away from the bright red flowers that were everywhere about; so presently her eyes grew heavy and she felt she must sit down to rest and to sleep. They kept walking until Dorothy could stand no longer. Her eyes closed in spite of herself and she forgot where she was and fell among the poppies." The Lion shouts, "The smell of the flowers is killing us all. I myself can scarcely keep my eyes open and the dog is asleep already."

The poppy field episode is rich with meaningful metaphoric imagery, and the film's portrayal of it highlights some important points. When Dorothy loses consciousness in the field the Lion lies down and goes to sleep. The Tin Man realizes, "It's the Wicked Witch!" and like a dam bursting with emotion begins calling for help. The Scarecrow says to the Tin Man, "It's no use screaming at a time like this! Nobody will hear you!" then himself begins shouting hysterically, "HELP! HELP! HELP!"

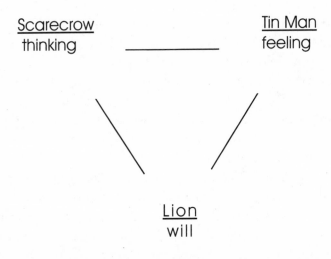

Scarecrow
thinking

Tin Man
feeling

Lion
will

The Unintegrated Soul

Cleverly illustrated here is what happens when the self loses consciousness and is no longer present to act as integrator of the threefold soul. Dorothy is knocked unconscious by the poppies and as a result the soul falls to pieces, each part polarizing in a different direction. The Scarecrow—Dorothy's thinking part, goes to one extreme, loosing power of sound thought and becoming hysterical. He no longer has Dorothy to keep him connected to the feelings and will, which he needs to help him stay grounded. The Tin Man—Dorothy's feeling part, also without Dorothy's presence, is left unchecked by clear thinking and the strength of the will. He becomes so awash in a sea of feelings he rusts himself again with his weeping. The Lion too is affected by the absence of the self, becoming asleep or inert. The will is overtaken by lethargy when thinking and feeling are no longer able to assist and motivate it into action.

This moment in the story captures in a simple picture something of great depth. It ingeniously shows the different soul states that result when the self and soul have not yet developed as a well-integrated unit. The challenges of life constantly test our development, as the poppy challenge does with Dorothy. Dorothy is overpowered by the poppies and her soul parts suffer the consequences. It is Dorothy who brought them together and without her, they fall apart. Fortunately, their call for help is heard.

In the film, the Good Witch appears to save the day. She is seen in the background waving her magic wand, making it snow to counteract the Witch's wicked doing. In the book, it is the Queen of the mice and her court who help them to escape the poppy field. (Baum added the snow idea himself when he turned *The Wizard of Oz* into a play in 1903). Both the Good Witch and the Queen Mouse are equally valid representations of the beneficent powers of life, overseeing and intervening at times to restore balance. When the Wicked Witch's plan is foiled she wretches scornfully, "Curses! Somebody always helps that girl!" This act of grace allows Dorothy to regain consciousness, regroup her soul parts and carry on with her journey.

Getting Off the Path

One may wonder how this collapse could have happened at all—Dorothy was given a kiss of protection from the Good Witch when she began her journey. Should that not have covered her for deadly poppies and witch's spells? There are several ways of examining this. The first is to say, it is simply because Dorothy *got off the path*. The group of them were no longer following the Yellow Brick Road, as Dorothy had been instructed. In the film, when they see the magnificence of the Emerald City in the distance, they are so thrilled at the sight of it, and so certain the Wizard will be able to help them, they decide to run through the poppy field. Of course this is the very thing the Wicked Witch wants. She has planted it there as a trap.

The moment Dorothy no longer heeds the Good Witch's directive to, "Just follow the Yellow Brick Road," she succumbs to the power that has been just waiting for a chance to take over. In the book it is even clearer. They end up on a river raft going the wrong way and this leads to the poppy field scenario. They want to get to the Emerald City but instead get, "farther and farther away from the road of yellow brick; and the water grew so deep that the long poles would not touch the bottom." When they got off the designated path, they literally got into deep water.

Lost in the Land of Oz, a great stork suddenly flies by and sees their plight. The stork asks, "Who are you and where are you going?" Dorothy answers, "We are going to the Emerald City." To this the stork replies, "This isn't the road." The stork points out to them that they are not on the right road to get where they want to go. This is just before they fall into the poppy field. They are not on the proper path and therefore vulnerable. It then takes *higher help* to rescue them from their folly. When they are finally clear of the poppy field Dorothy realizes, "We must journey on until we find the road of yellow brick again." Recognizing the need to make a correction in their direction, "it was not long before they reached the road of yellow brick and turned again towards the Emerald City where the great Oz dwelt."

We should keep in mind we are all going to trip off the path sometime. We are all going to make wrong turns. That is part of being human. We would have to be born perfect to avoid slipping up. But to work on our imperfections is precisely why we were born. So we should expect to make mistakes, acknowledge them as opportunities for learning, and receive the wisdom inherent in them once we turn them inside out.

The possibility of getting off the path is an important consideration of the journey. This is where our freedom is observed. If we remember back to when Dorothy first set foot on the Yellow Brick Road, there were other roads she could have taken. There are always other options to follow. Life often presents us with crossroads and not every road leads in the same direction. This is the case so that every person is free to choose what direction they wish to go—or not go.

The Power of Illusion

One could ask why Dorothy and her companions got off the path and into the poppy field? Why did they stray from the Yellow Brick Road? The poppy field represents the power of illusion. It appeared as one thing, but turned out to be something quite different.

There are many illusions and countless distractions to seduce us off the path and lead us astray. We all face poppies on the path. Illusions appear to us one way but in reality are something of a different nature. They often have unexpected, if not unpleasant effects once we step into them. In the Oz story, what appeared at first as beautiful turned out to be poison. Its attractiveness camouflaged its deadliness.

Illusion, or *Maya* as it is called in Eastern teachings, has the power to trap us by our own senses. The Witch trapped them with something, "attractive to the eye and soothing to the smell." Dorothy's initial reaction to the flowers was, "Aren't they beautiful?" as she breathed in the spicy scent of the flowers. We can be easily deceived by our senses. What is required, to protect ourselves, is that we use more than our senses in making our way along the path of life. We need to employ our greater powers. In doing so we can overcome the power of illusion rather than the power of illusion overcoming us. We need to grow beyond our naive state of mind and act with greater prudence. It is in the using of our powers that the antidote to illusion is found. There we will find what will avert us from errors on the path of life.

As for Dorothy, she is still unawake to the power she possesses. As a result, she literally fell for the illusion and was no longer able to act as integrator of the soul parts, and they in turn fell apart. The poppy field almost put an end to her journey and her soul parts' dreams of fulfillment.

Poppies: Helpful or Harmful?

It is no accident that Baum used poppies in this story. Around the time of his writing *The Wizard of Oz*, poppies were popular as the source of a legal form of opium. The word "poppy" comes from the Latin, "papaver," referring to the *pap* or juice from the flower that was served to babies for centuries to help them sleep. The ancient Greeks, who thought sleep the greatest of all remedies, drank large amounts of poppy juice and dedicated the flower to the Gods of sleep. For over five thousand years the *pap of the poppy* has been used as a sedative in the form of opium, morphine and heroin. But because of its addictive nature and subsequent abuse, its legal use has become largely restricted to medical purposes only, for which it still has value.

Like many things in life the power of the poppies is a two-edged sword. It is both beneficial and deadly, *helpful* and *harmful*. It all depends on the context and intention of its use. The Wicked Witch was obviously not out to help Dorothy, but rather to harm her. Her intention with the poppies was to enchant Dorothy with something "with poison in it," and to put her to sleep. The Wicked Witch wanted Dorothy to lose consciousness.

Consciousness is power and the power of the self is in its consciousness. By losing consciousness rather than gaining it, Dorothy received the opposite of what the journey could give her. Losing consciousness, she lost control. The soul parts then became worse off than they were before. They were engaged but unguarded. Without Dorothy's presence the soul parts were left vulnerable to oppressive powers to take over and enslave them, as they feared the Wicked Witch would do. This is a very real example of the destructive effects drug abuse can have on a person.

Drugs can give the *illusion* of consciousness. They can induce a sense of enhanced selfhood, but in reality subvert the self. The drug takes the self on a "trip," and in fact takes the place of the self. Drugs knock the self out and undermine the power of true consciousness with a drug-induced consciousness. But this form of consciousness has not been earned through proper preparation and self-development, and therefore is not under the control of the self.

Many people use drugs to get "high." But as Dorothy follows the guidance of the Good Witch—following the Yellow Brick Road, it has not initially got her "high" or taken her to the heights. Rather it has taken her down and in, to the "dark and creepy" places of herself. Reaching the heights comes later, after the preparatory groundwork has been done. Drugs, in the end, do not take a person to the real high places of life, but rather brings them to a place even lower than where they were before. It is exchanging one dependency for another.

To find the real highs of life, what the Good Witch told Dorothy is the best guidance to follow. In Munchkinland when Dorothy asked, "How do I start for the Emerald City?" the Good Witch advised, "It's always best to start at the beginning." Of course, but what is the beginning? How does one get started?

Where you are at any given moment is always the starting point. And every step is a new beginning. The key is to be true to where you are, because you can't move from anywhere other than where you are. Where you are right now is your next beginning point. It seems obvious, but people try all the time to move from somewhere other than where they really are, and jump over steps and stages to get where they think they want to go. This only compounds their lostness and detours the journey.

Instead of working with *where* they are and *what* they are, following the Yellow Brick Road as it unfolds itself before them, drugs cause a person to skip over important steps and stages, taking them in a different direction. Taking drugs is choosing another road, rather than the Yellow Brick Road—as if there were a shortcut home. But the idea that there are shortcuts is also an illusion.

Dorothy's longing for somewhere over the rainbow is a yearning for color in her life amidst a gray world. Even though drugs do bring a certain coloring to our lives, we should consider if that is the source of color from which we want to draw. As for Dorothy, the poppies "were so brilliant in color they almost dazzled Dorothy's eyes." But because of her naivete, they almost killed her. It was illusion's deadly trap. There is an alternative to taking psychedelics if we want more color in our lives. If we instead stay on the Yellow Brick Road and patiently pursue the steps of personal development it leads us through, it will bring color to our life *naturally*, and take us to the highest points possible.

Awakening with Greater Wisdom

As we follow the *longing of life*, we will find overcoming illusions and addictions of all kinds is a part of the journey. The ability to do this lies in our own power. It means awakening from our spiritual slumber and seeing our lives within a bigger picture—one that includes a spiritual context. Only that will help us successfully meet the trials and challenges.

Dorothy has successfully passed though many challenges so far. The poppy field almost ended her journey but fortunately recovery was possible. With some help, Dorothy regained consciousness and with that, awakened with greater wisdom about the nature of the journey and the need to stay on the path. But her journey home is far from over. Other opportunities to overcome illusion will arise. Even her idea about "home" must undergo the test for *illusion*.

5

The Emerald City

"Come on, lets get out of here!" says Dorothy to her traveling companions as they leave the poppy field behind and get back on the Yellow Brick Road. The poppy ordeal over, Dorothy, the Scarecrow, Tin Man, Lion and Toto proceed on the last leg of the journey to find the Wizard of Oz. In the book they meet some of the local residents on their approach to the Emerald City.

"Once more they could see fences built beside the road; but these were painted green, and when they came to a small house, in which a farmer evidently lived, that also was painted green. The people were all dressed in clothing of a lovely emerald green color and wore peaked hats like those of the Munchkins." The Scarecrow points out, "Everything is green here, while in the country of the Munchkins blue was the favorite color." Dorothy is meeting more colors as she explores her inner realm.

The Scarecrow voices a concern, "The people do not seem to be as friendly as the Munchkins and I'm afraid we shall be unable to find a place to pass the night." Dorothy walks boldly up to a large farmhouse and knocks on the door. When a woman answers, Dorothy inquires if they can spend the night there. After taking a good look at the strange crew of characters standing outside her door, the woman invites them in to give them supper and a place to sleep.

Once inside they meet the rest of the family and learn more about the mysterious Wizard of Oz. When asked why they want to see the Wizard, who apparently no one has ever seen, they each share what it is they wish of him. "I want him to give me some brains," says the Scarecrow eagerly. "And I want him to give me a heart," says the Tin Man. "And I want him to give me courage," says the Cowardly Lion. "And I want him to send me back to Kansas," says Dorothy, who could not explain where Kansas is, except to say that it is where her home is. "The next morning, as soon as the sun was up, they started on their way, and soon saw a beautiful green glow in the sky just before them. 'That must be the Emerald City,' said Dorothy. As they walked on, the green glow became brighter and brighter and it seemed that at last they were nearing the end of the travels."

The Guardian of the Gates

Entering the Emerald City takes some effort. "In front of them, at the end of the road of yellow brick, was a big gate, all studded with emeralds that glittered so in the sun that even the painted eyes of the Scarecrow were dazzled by their brilliancy. There was a bell beside the gate, and Dorothy pushed the button and heard a silvery tinkle sound within." When the door swings open they come face to face with "the guardian of the gates," after whom this particular chapter of Baum's book is named. "When he saw Dorothy and her companions the man asked, 'What do you wish in the Emerald City?' 'We came to see the Great Oz,' said Dorothy. The man was so surprised at this answer that he sat down to think it over."

The greeting they receive in the film, with all the nonsense about the sign that reads, "Bell out of order. Please knock!" starts to tip them off that there is something a little odd about this place and things may not be quite as they expected. The guardian is reluctant at first to let them in, but after they inform him that the Good Witch sent them, and prove it by pointing out the magic slippers, they are allowed to enter.

The first matter at hand is for each of them to put on a pair of spectacles. Glasses with green colored lenses are to be locked on, as the Wizard of Oz has ordered, and the guardian is the only keeper of the key. The reason given is that the "brightness and glory of the Emerald City" would otherwise be blinding. The group of them are then lead through the streets of the Emerald City where everything appears with a green tint. "The window panes were of green glass; even the sky above the City had a green tint, and the rays of the sun were green." As they follow the guardian, they get a good look at the apparently green people, with their green clothes and green food, who in turn stop and stare at Dorothy and her strangely assorted company.

In the film they are taken to the Wash & Brush Up Company to tidy up a bit. When finished there, they merrily make their last steps to see the Wizard. But suddenly confusion breaks out when the Wicked Witch of the West makes an appearance overhead on her broomstick. She does some skywriting, sending the message, "SURRENDER DOROTHY." The poppy field trap didn't work for her, so perhaps she can intimidate Dorothy into surrendering. Everyone goes rushing to the door of the Wizard's palace to seek his counsel. The guard calms them and sends them all home—all except Dorothy and her companions, who are now even more anxious to see the Wizard.

Again they meet with resistance. They point out that Dorothy is the one to whom the Wicked Witch is sending the message. That changes things for the guard who tells them to wait while he goes and announces them to the Wizard. This certainly peaks their hopes and the Scarecrow says, "I've as good as got my brain!" The Tin Man says, "I can fairly hear my heart beating!" Dorothy adds excitedly, "I'll be home in time for supper!" And the Lion finalizes, "In another hour I'll be King of the Forest. Long live the King!" at which point he does his entertaining song about the virtues of courage.

The guard finally returns and reports that the Wizard has said for them to go away. Their hopes are dashed. The Scarecrow comments, "Looks like we came a long way for nothing." This sends Dorothy into tears as she sits down on the steps. Something comes next in the film which, like many parts of the film happens very quickly— adding up to seconds rather than minutes, but speaks volumes when one thinks about it.

Penitence on the Path

What Dorothy does at this point amplifies a significant and noteworthy point. It illustrates something that is not necessarily a popular notion in our modern culture, but is nonetheless an important quality. It is one in which serious seekers who wish to make headway on the homeward journey need to consider.

Faced with an apparently hopeless situation, Dorothy enters a state of sorrow. This is not just because she has been refused entry to see the Wizard and is feeling sorry for herself. But rather it is over things of her past, which she begins to reflect upon. Spontaneously she shares with the others, "Auntie Em was so good to me and I never appreciated it, running away and hurting her feelings. Professor Marvel said she was sick. She may be dying! And it's all my fault. Oh I'll never forgive myself! Never—never—never!"

What she shares with the others amounts to a confession, and regret for wrongdoing. The closing of this door in the Emerald City has put her into an inner space where she faces shame over forgotten aspects of her life. It is secondary what the content of her confession is—that in a sense reveals more naivete. The important point is the process she enters at this time. One could call it, "a period of penitence on the path," penitence meaning "sorrow for wrongdoing and a willingness to make amends." What follows from this is also noteworthy. Something shifts. We see the guard moved to tears as he tells Dorothy she can now come in to see the Wizard, and the door swings open.

The underlying message of these moments on the steps is that, where and how our journey goes is directly dependent upon our attitude. *Attitude determines outcome.* The refused entry at the gates of the Wizard's palace put Dorothy into an attitude of humility. It triggered sincere remorse for shortcomings of the past. She took the time to go though some self-examination and openly admit her guilt. Sometimes we have to look back in order to move forward. It was no doubt painful while it lasted, but it was soon over and a door that was otherwise closed opened for her.

It is interesting that it isn't perfection that allowed Dorothy admittance. Traveling the Yellow Brick Road is not about being perfect, but rather about finding the right relationship to our imperfections. It is not our humanness that blocks our way, but our refusal to own what is ours in our evolving human nature. Denial of the truth about ourselves may give us a temporary sense of okayness, but the capacity for *healthy* shame is a far more valuable commodity. It is the willingness to admit, with brutal honesty, the truth about our life and where we are on the journey, that clears the way. A humble disposition will empower us in ways we can hardly imagine and open many doors that would otherwise be closed due to a prideful disposition.

Religious tradition speaks of how the act of repentance leads to atonement or at-one-ment; a reunion with the divine. Even though Dorothy said, "Oh I'll never forgive myself!" it appears her penitence shifted something in the surrounding circumstance and the obstruction was lifted—a sign of forgiveness. Dorothy's attitude also shows the importance of love on the path. Love means we are willing to say we are sorry. When we find it within ourselves to develop the attitude Dorothy illustrates here, we too will find doors opening—doors we perhaps did not even know existed.

All this speaks again of how the journey is not necessarily all gaiety and high-flying but may require periods of painful inner work. Like Cinderella, we can don rags and go down into the cinders, to sift through the ashes and pick through the details of our life. There the pearls of wisdom and true treasures are to be found. A time of *sackcloth and ashes* can be the very thing we need to renew our strength for what lies ahead. It is taking time to contemplate our unworthiness, that prepares us for the greatness that is calling us from the future. Then as we rise out of the ashes we find ourselves empowered with new vision, and new vistas opening up—as was the case with Dorothy. Following this, Dorothy finally gets in to meet the Wizard of Oz.

Meeting the Wizard

In the book, each of the four has to enter the presence of the Wizard on their own to make their request. They are all given the same answer—they must do something to earn the right before he will do anything for them. He tells them they must first prove themselves *worthy* by performing a very small task. They are instructed to kill the Wicked Witch of the West. In addition, they are told to bring back her broomstick as proof of the deed.

The Lion asks the question, "But what if she kills us first?" When the Wizard booms his response, "Bring me the broomstick of the Wicked Witch of the West!" the Lion is quite a sight as he goes running down the hall, crashing through a pane of glass. Dorothy's courage literally goes flying out the window.

More than a "small task," this is quite a challenge that the Wizard presents to them. It is more like the *ultimate challenge*. Dorothy was quite frightened by her first encounter with the Wicked Witch of the West, back in Munchkinland. Having to go and kill her is a terrifying prospect. Dorothy has been willing enough to follow the

Yellow Brick Road, as instructed by the Good Witch, but this is not a part of the journey she was counting on. Is it really necessary?

When Dorothy is told by the Wizard that she must kill the Wicked Witch of the West she protests, "But I cannot!" The Wizard responds matter-of-factly, "You killed the Witch of the East and you wear the silver shoes which bear a powerful charm." These are points that Dorothy is not bearing much in mind yet—which is precisely why *it is* necessary for her to have this further challenge. She needs to become more aware of her own power.

The killing of the first witch, the Witch of the East, took initiative, but happened with little or no deliberateness on Dorothy's part. It was more the result of reacting to threatening circumstances in Kansas, than a conscious decision. She told the Munchkins, "It was an accident." The task of facing the Wicked Witch of the West will give Dorothy the opportunity to take further initiative, but this time with consciousness and deliberateness—purposely putting her power to work. Not until she does this will she be able to go home. As the Wizard states, "Until the Wicked Witch dies you will not see your uncle and aunt again!"

6

Facing the Witch

Reluctant to do what the Wizard demanded, but seeing no other way to get what they came for, the four resolve to band together to complete their assigned task. "Therefore it was decided to start upon their journey the next morning, and the Woodman sharpened his axe on a green grindstone and had all his joints properly oiled. The Scarecrow stuffed himself with fresh straw and Dorothy put new paint on his eyes that he might see better. The green girl, who was very kind to them, filled Dorothy's basket with good things to eat, and fastened a little bell around Toto's neck with a green ribbon."

Lead by a green soldier they return to where they first entered the Emerald City. As they are being let through the gate, Dorothy asks, "Which road leads to the Wicked Witch of the West?" "There is no road," answers the Guardian of the Gates. "No one ever wishes to go that way." "How then will we find her?" inquires Dorothy.

After they explain the purpose of their mission is to find the Witch and destroy her, the Guardian instructs them, "Keep to the west, where the sun sets, and you cannot fail to find her." And so they venture west in search of the Wicked Witch of the West.

The Orientation of Oz

Becoming oriented to the inner world is part of the process of the journey. To help with this, Dorothy is at least afforded the four cardinal directions—east, west, north and south. Oz has all four, with the Emerald City at the center.

There are four witches altogether in this other world, each named after the area they live in. The Wicked Witch of the East was destroyed at the beginning with the landing of Dorothy's house, and whose magic slippers she now wears. The Wicked Witch of the West is related to the Witch of the East, as we heard when she said, "Who killed my sister?" There is also the Witch of the north whom Dorothy met in Munchkinland and one of the south—both good witches.

The Transformational Day

Dorothy's journey in the Land of Oz began in the east. She has made it to the center of Oz—the Emerald City. Now she must continue traveling to the other side of Oz to deal with the Witch of the West. Her journey takes her from east to west—the same way the sun travels on its daily path.

Dorothy's journey is a metaphor for what could be called the *Transformational Day*. The Transformational Day is another name for the archetypal path of the life journey we all follow. Dorothy's transformation of the

Wicked Witch of the East was the sunrise of her Transformational Day, or the dawning of her consciousness. Transforming the Wicked Witch of the West will be the sunset or close of her Transformational Day. The first witch was transformed with little or no consciousness. By the end of the day Dorothy must face the other wicked witch with full consciousness.

Dorothy's journey is a metaphor for something that is an ongoing pattern for everyone. Like Dorothy, we are all somewhere in the cycle between the sunrise and sunset of the Transformational Day, the developing of consciousness. This process is taking place in every situation, everyday of our lives. The story line of *The Wizard of Oz* gives us a map with which we can track ourselves on this journey.

The Transformational Day is about transforming ourselves as dependent beings into independent beings, through the development of our consciousness. We begin life with little consciousness and complete dependency on those around us. We rely on others to do for us what we cannot do for ourselves, including carrying our soul life—our thinking, feeling and will.

Dependency is justified to a certain point. We are all dependent on others to some degree. But dependency can turn into oppression if we remain with what we have outgrown. Once we have the capacity to do more for ourselves, we are responsible to do so. As our soul grows, and with that our consciousness, we become capable of doing more for ourselves. We become more dependent in ourselves or *independent.* To get to this place, as with Dorothy, we are required to follow the course of the transformational process, or "live out" the Transformational Day—moving from a place of little consciousness to one of full consciousness. In doing so we must overcome dependencies that would become oppressive. And to do that we must use our powers and capabilities.

Dorothy has made steps toward this goal, overcoming aspects of dependency in her life that otherwise would have become oppressive. She accomplished this in the outer realm, not only with Miss Gulch, but from outgrown dependency on Auntie Em and Uncle Henry—as symbolized in the death of the Wicked Witch of the East. But now she faces the greatest challenge of all. To seek out the Wicked Witch of the West with full consciousness, and destroy her. This is the direction she needs to follow to reach the other side of the Transformational Day and to become a free and independent being.

The Witch Finds Them

"The Emerald City was soon left far behind. As they advanced, the ground became rougher and hillier, for there were no farms nor houses in this country of the West, and the ground was untilled." As Dorothy continues Westward she is breaking new ground in yet unexplored areas of herself.

It is not long before the Wicked Witch of the West sees them coming. She has but one eye, with telescopic power that allows her to see everywhere. This is a characteristic Hollywood left out. Instead, the film Witch sees them coming in her crystal ball.

Intending to make short their visit, the Witch blows once on a silver whistle around her neck. "At once there came running to her from all directions a pack of great wolves. They had long legs and fierce eyes and sharp teeth." The Witch commands them to go and tear the bunch of them to pieces. As they are seen dashing toward them the Tin Man says, "This is my fight!" and tells the rest to get behind him. Impassioned by the attack, and with his newly sharpened axe in hand, he begins swinging. "There were forty wolves, and forty times a wolf was killed, so that at last they all lay dead in a heap."

This enrages the Witch who then blows on her whistle two times. "Straightway a great flock of wild crows came flying towards her, enough to darken the sky." The Witch commands them to fly to the strangers, peck out their eyes and tear them to pieces. With this onslaught the Scarecrow says, "This is my battle, so lie down beside me and you will not be harmed." This is quite a statement from a Scarecrow who back in the cornfield thought himself powerless against the birds. But he succeeds in fending off the crows and protecting his companions. "There were forty crows, and forty times the Scarecrow twisted a neck, until at last all were lying dead beside him."

This only angers the Witch more, who next blows on her whistle three times. "Forthwith there was heard a great buzzing in the air, and a swarm of black bees came flying towards her. 'Go to the strangers and sting them to death!'" commands the Witch. Upon this attack the Tin Man and the Scarecrow work together relentlessly until they have destroyed all the Witch's bees. "The Wicked Witch was so angry when she saw her black bees in little heaps like fine coal that she stamped her foot and tore her hair and gnashed her teeth. And then she called a dozen of her slaves, who were the Winkies, and gave them sharp spears, telling them to go to the strangers and destroy them." This time it is the Lion's turn to save the day who "gave a great roar and sprang towards them, and the poor Winkies were so frightened that they ran as fast as they could." Not bad for a cowardly lion. The three soul parts are getting opportunities to exercise their abilities.

Their success has greatly reduced the Wicked Witch's options. But not about to give up she "sat down to think what she should do next. She could not understand how all her plans to destroy these strangers had failed; but she was a powerful Witch, as well as a wicked one, and she soon made up her mind how to act."

The Witch has in her possession a Golden Cap with a magic charm to it. "Whoever owned it could call three times upon the Winged Monkeys, who would obey any order they were given. But no person could command these strange creatures more than three times. Twice already the Wicked Witch had used the charm of the Cap. Once was when she made the Winkies her slaves, and set herself to rule over their country. The Winged Monkeys had helped her to do this. The second time was when she had fought against the Great Oz himself, and driven him out of the land of the West. The Winged Monkeys had also helped her in doing this. Only once more could she use this Golden Cap, for which reason she did not like to do so until all her other powers were exhausted. But now that her fierce wolves and her wild crows and her stinging bees were gone, and her slaves had been scared away by the Cowardly Lion, she saw there was only one way left to destroy Dorothy and her friends."

After repeating an incantation and making some magical gestures the charm begins to work. "The sky was darkened, and a low rumbling sound was heard in the air. There was a rushing of many wings, a great chattering and laughing, and the sun came out of the dark sky to show the Wicked Witch surrounded by a crowd of monkeys, each with a pair of immense and powerful wings on his shoulders. One, much bigger than the others, seemed to be their leader. He flew close to the Witch and said, 'You have called us for the third and last time. What do you command?'"

This is where the film picks up the story, leaving nothing to the imagination with its depiction of these disturbing looking creatures. The film is different in that the Witch tells the Winged Monkeys to bring Dorothy and Toto back to her, whereas in the book she tells the Monkeys to destroy them all except the Lion, whom she wants to use for a workhorse. The Lion is brought to the Witch and tied up in a small yard with a high iron fence around it. As the leader of the Winged Monkeys flies toward Dorothy to destroy her, "his long, hairy arms stretched out and his ugly face grinning terribly; he saw the mark of the Good Witch's kiss upon her forehead and stopped short, motioning to the others not to touch her. 'We dare not harm this little girl,' he said to them, 'for she is protected by the Power of Good, and that is greater than the Power of Evil. All we can do is carry her to the castle of the Wicked Witch and leave her there.'" And so Dorothy and Toto are taken to the Witch's Castle.

Captive in the Witch's Castle

The Witch surveys the situation. "The Wicked Witch was both surprised and worried when she saw the mark on Dorothy's forehead. At first the Witch was tempted to run away from Dorothy; but she happened to look into the child's eyes and saw how simple the soul behind them was, and that the little girl did not know of the wonderful power the Silver Shoes gave her. So the

Wicked Witch laughed to herself, and thought, 'I can still make her my slave, for she does not know how to use her power.'" The Witch preys on Dorothy's lingering innocence.

The Witch puts Dorothy to work as a kitchen slave, threatening her with death if she doesn't follow everything she is told. Dorothy yields to the Witch's intimidation. She is helpless at this point, as she truly does not know how to use the power at her disposal. "Dorothy went to work meekly, with her mind made up to work as hard as she could; for she was glad the Wicked Witch had decided not to kill her." Dorothy is caught midstream between naivete and knowledge, and therefore enslavement has become her lot.

Meanwhile, the Lion is acting anything but cowardly as the Witch tries to harness him like a horse. "But as she opened the gate the Lion gave a loud roar and bounded at her so fiercely that the Witch was afraid, and ran out and shut the gate again." Even Toto resists the Witch's intimidation tactics. "Once the Witch struck Toto a blow with her umbrella and the brave little dog flew at her and bit her leg in return. The Witch did not bleed where she was bitten, for she was so wicked that the blood in her had dried up many years before."

In the film, the Witch puts Toto in a basket and plans to destroy him by having him drowned in the river. But he climbs out of the basket and escapes from the castle. What follows at this point demonstrates well the soul parts in action. The three soul parts are outside the Witch's Castle, wondering what to do when Toto finds them. The Tin Man says, "Look! There's Toto! Where'd he come from?" The Scarecrow, the thinking part, clues in and says, "Why, don't you see? He's come to take us to Dorothy!" As they begin to follow Toto, we see them making their way up a rocky climb. The two others being pulled by the Lion's tail, the Lion provides the *will* power to get them up the steep and dangerous trek. Where there's a will, there's a way.

When they reach the top and get a closer look at the Witch's Castle, the Tin Man, the heart, becomes emotional and cries, "Oh, I hate to think of her in there. We've got to get her out!" Then the brains of the bunch, the Scarecrow, says, "I've got a plan how to get in there." Looking at the Lion he tells him, "And you're gonna lead us."

This shows wonderfully how the threefold soul works together. When the heart is moved to do something, as the Tin Man is, the head figures out how to do it, as the Scarecrow does, and then it is handed over to the will to put it into action. It takes all three.

Of course the will, or Lion needs a few moments to muster his courage. Finally he agrees, "All right, I'll go in there for Dorothy—Wicked Witch or no Wicked Witch—guards or no guards—I'll tear 'em apart—Woof! I may not come out alive, but I'm going in there!" Then he makes the comical comment, "There's only one thing I want you fellas to do." "What's that?" they ask. "Talk me out of it!"

Here we see a characteristic of the will, with its swinging between pride and fear, overconfidence and underconfidence. We also see how without the work of the will, the cleverest of ideas or the most passionate of feelings remain unrealized. All three faculties need to work together. Here the three soul components rally together and rather than becoming slaves to the Wicked Witch, they serve the self.

The Shoe Down

"Now the Wicked Witch had a great longing to have for her own the Silver Shoes which the girl always wore. Her bees and her crows and her wolves were lying in heaps and drying up, and she had used up all the power of the Golden Cap; but if she could only get hold of the Silver Shoes they would give her more power than all the other things she had lost. She watched Dorothy carefully, to see if she ever took off her shoes, thinking she might steal them. But the child was so proud of her pretty shoes that she never took them off except at night and when she took her bath. The Witch was too much afraid of the dark to dare go in Dorothy's room at night to take the shoes, and her dread of water was greater than her fear of the dark, so she never came near when Dorothy was bathing. But the wicked creature was very cunning, and she finally thought of a trick that would give her what she wanted."

The Witch decides to put an iron bar in the middle of the floor, then with her magic arts makes it invisible. When Dorothy walks by she trips on it and falls. "She was not much hurt, but in her fall one of the Silver Shoes came off, and before she could reach it the Wicked Witch had snatched it away and put it on her own skinny foot. The wicked woman was greatly pleased with the success of her trick, for as long as she had one of the shoes she owned half the power of their charm, and Dorothy could not use it against her, even had she known how to do so."

Dorothy is being anything but successful in complet-ing her assignment to destroy the Wicked Witch of the West. So far she has been separated from her soul parts, submitted to the Witch's enslavement, lost one of her magic shoes and is halfway to being destroyed herself. The words of the Good Witch must have echoed in Dorothy's ears at this moment, reminding her to never let the magic slippers off her feet, or she would be at the mercy of the Wicked Witch. In other words—*Never give up your power!*

Suddenly a turning takes place in Dorothy. She becomes very vocal about what is rightfully hers. "The little girl seeing she had lost one of her pretty shoes grew angry and said to the Witch, 'Give me back my shoe!' 'I will not,' retorted the Witch, 'for it is now my shoe and not yours.' 'You are a wicked creature!' cried Dorothy. 'You have no right to take my shoe from me.' 'I shall keep it just the same,' said the Witch, laughing at her, 'and some day I shall get the other from you too.'"

What follows is dramatically different in the film as compared with the book. In the film, the three soul parts attempt to rescue Dorothy but are taken captive with her. All end up at the mercy of the Wicked Witch. The Witch starts the process of destroying them by igniting her broomstick and then lighting the Scarecrow on fire. To save the Scarecrow, Dorothy grabs a nearby bucket of water. The Witch screams, "Don't touch that water!" But when Dorothy throws it over the Scarecrow, some splashes on the Witch. Within seconds, to everyone's astonishment, she begins to melt away until there is nothing left of her. Afterwards Dorothy says she didn't mean to kill the Witch. This does not nearly show the strengthened selfhood that comes through in Baum's version.

In the book, Dorothy's deed takes place in a different way. Dorothy becomes incensed by the Witch's trick to get her shoe. "This made Dorothy so very angry that she picked up the bucket of water that stood near and dashed it over the Witch, wetting her from head to foot. Instantly the wicked woman gave a loud cry of fear, and then, as Dorothy looked at her in wonder, the Witch began to shrink and fall away. 'See what you have done!' she screamed. 'In a minute I shall melt away.' With these words the Witch fell down in a brown, melted, shapeless mass and began to spread over the clean boards of the kitchen floor." And so Dorothy deliberately does away with the Witch.

The main difference in the book is that Dorothy has clearly had enough of the old Witch and decides to do something about it. It is her turn to get angry—and she does, giving it to the Witch. She first finds her voice, then her power, which she blasts at the Witch with a bucket of water. She is fully conscious about what she is doing and deliberately picks up the bucket to throw at the Witch. The words of the Good Witch must have sparked the fighting spirit in Dorothy and made her realize she was going to have to take a stand. Even with only one shoe on she finds the strength to stand up for herself and dowse this oppressive part. It of course was her intention to do away with the Witch. To destroy the Wicked Witch was her assigned task, not an accident as implied by the film.

Washed Away With Water

The Witch is washed away with water. L. Frank Baum's use of water is quite in line with the symbolism of water found in many traditions, both ancient and modern. Water is obviously something that is suggestive of cleansing—we use it for physical cleansing. John the Baptist took people into the river as a gesture symbolic of spiritual cleansing. Dorothy's use of water symbolizes a cleansing, purifying and transforming of this spiritual influence in her life.

Water is also symbolic of consciousness. Some consider a body of water and what lies below its surface to represent the unconscious. One could say Dorothy's reaching for a bucket of water is symbolic of her taking hold of her unconscious resources. It indicates an expansion of consciousness to include the use of power that was hitherto untapped.

The Witch had an aversion to water knowing it was the one thing that could put an end to her. Which is to say, Dorothy's conscious use of power was the only thing that would arrest the Witch's oppressive influence. Dorothy discovered her power and with that literally washed the Witch away.

Dorothy's action shows proaction—one bucket was not enough. She continues with more water on the Witch. "Seeing that she had really melted away to nothing, Dorothy drew another bucket of water and threw it over the mess. She then swept it all out of the door." If one is going to do an assigned task, one may as well make sure it is complete. "After picking out the silver shoe, which was all that was left of the old woman, she cleaned and dried it with a cloth and put it on her foot again. Then at last being free to do as she chose, she ran out to the courtyard to tell the Lion that the Wicked Witch of the West had come to an end, and that they were no longer prisoners in a strange land."

Dorothy informs the Winkies they too are no longer slaves to the Wicked Witch. Dorothy's sense of self must have grown immensely in those moments. I imagine her walking out the door, both shoes on, her head held high, announcing to everyone they have been set free. "There was great rejoicing among the yellow Winkies, for they had been made to work hard during many years for the Wicked Witch, who had always treated them with great cruelty." And just as the Mayor of Munchkinland had declared it a "day of independence," at the beginning of the Transformational Day, when Dorothy destroyed the Wicked Witch of the East, so too the Winkies proclaim it a special day to commemorate the end of the Wicked Witch of the West. "They kept this day as a holiday, then and ever after, and spent the time in feasting and dancing."

Together Again

After having been separated for a time, Dorothy and her threefold soul are joined back together again. The triumph over the Witch has actually forged an even greater bond between each of the soul parts and with Dorothy. The Tin Man is "so pleased that he wept tears of joy. Now that they were reunited, Dorothy and her friends spent a few happy days at the Yellow Castle, where they found everything they needed to make them comfortable. But one day the girl thought of Aunt Em and said, 'We must go back to Oz and claim his promise.' 'Yes,' said the Woodman, 'at last I shall get my heart.' 'And I shall get my brains,' added the Scarecrow joyfully. 'And I shall get my courage,' said the Lion thoughtfully. 'And I shall get back to Kansas,' cried Dorothy, clapping her hands. 'Oh, let us start for the Emerald City tomorrow!'"

Scarecrow
thinking

Tin Man
feeling

Dorothy
self

Lion
will

Dorothy and the Threefold Soul

7

Confronting the Wizard

Back to the Emerald City

As Dorothy and her companions prepare for their journey back to the Emerald City, they say their good-byes to the Winkies. The Winkies are sorry to see them go, but are nonetheless grateful for their coming. "Then, being prepared for the journey, they all started for the Emerald City; and the Winkies gave them three cheers and many good wishes to carry with them."

Getting back to the Emerald City presents another challenge. Baum points out, "You will remember there was no road—not even a pathway—between the castle of the Wicked Witch and the Emerald City. When the four travelers went in search of the Witch she had seen them coming, and so sent the Winged Monkeys to bring them to her. They knew of course, they must go straight east, towards the rising sun, and they started off in the right way." They make a good start, but after awhile find their journey is going nowhere.

Even though it is apparent they are lost, Dorothy tries to remain optimistic, "If we walk far enough we shall sometime come to some place, I am sure." But despite her assurance, this philosophy does not prove to work. "Day by day passed away, and they still saw nothing before them but the scarlet fields." The Scarecrow begins to grumble a bit. "We have surely lost our way, and unless we find it again in time to reach the Emerald City I shall never get my brains." The rest grumble along with him. The glory of their victory is gone and now they are concerned that they may never receive their rewards.

After some deliberation, Dorothy comes to the realization that she can use the Golden Cap she brought with her from the Witch's castle. Inside the cap is conveniently written the directions for using its power. By using the magic of the Golden Cap, Dorothy is becoming more adept at using the power available to her. Within moments the Winged Monkeys show up and oblige her request to be flown back to the Emerald City.

Bringing Back the Broom

Entering the Emerald City, they again must have glasses locked on. Everyone is surprised to see them, as their return was not expected. But they are treated with great respect once the word spreads that Dorothy has melted the Wicked Witch. "The soldier had the news carried straight to Oz that Dorothy and the other travelers had come back again, after destroying the Wicked Witch; but Oz made no reply. They thought the Great Oz would send for them at once, but he did not. They had no word from him the next day, nor the next, nor the next."

This starts to kindle Dorothy's anger again. She feels this is rather poor treatment from the Wizard, after risking life and limb to complete the mission he gave them. So she sends a strong message to him with the green girl, telling him she is going to call on the Winged Monkeys to help her find out if he keeps his promises or not. Next morning—no problem—they are in there first thing. Dorothy does it again.

After they inform the Wizard what has become of the Witch, they remind him of his promises. "You promised to send me back to Kansas," says Dorothy. "And you promised to give me brains," says the Scarecrow. "And you promised to give me a heart," says the Tin Man. "And you promised to give me courage," says the Lion. There is some hesitation by the Wizard, and then he tells them to come back tomorrow. But not wanting to wait a moment longer they stand their ground. The Lion exercises more of his courage and gives a mighty roar. It is so fierce it even frightens Toto, who jumps in alarm, knocking a screen over. This reveals a funny little man standing behind it. In the film, while Dorothy is protesting the Wizard's response, Toto pulls a curtain aside, exposing the Wizard at his tricks. In either case, it is once again one of Toto's serendipitous acts that brings new direction to the situation.

The Not-So-Wonderful Wizard of Oz

Wanting to know exactly what is going on, they demand an explanation from this man. He confesses that he is the one and only *Wizard of Oz*, and everything has been a great charade of his. "I'm just a common man," he concedes. Stripped of his mask, the table is now turned on the Wizard. "You're more than that," says the Scarecrow in a grieved tone, "You're a humbug." The Wizard agrees quickly to this.

After explaining to them how he does some of his tricks and created such a facade, he begins to tell them the story of how it all came to be. They hear the details of his accidental decent by balloon into this strange and beautiful place, and how the awestruck people dubbed him, "the Wizard of Oz." "Times being what they were, I accepted the job," he bemuses.

He further explains, "Just to amuse myself, and keep the good people busy, I ordered them to build this City, and my Palace; and they did it willingly and well. Then I thought, as the country was so green and beautiful, I would call it the Emerald City, and to make the name fit better I put green spectacles on all the people, so that everything they saw was green." Shocked by this revelation Dorothy asks, "But isn't everything here green?" "No more than in any other city," replies the Wizard, "But when you wear green spectacles, why of course everything you see looks green to you."

This explains why, when Dorothy left the Emerald City to find the Wicked Witch and took off the spectacles, "the pretty silk dress she had put on in the palace, to her surprise, she found was no longer green, but pure white. The ribbon around Toto's neck had also lost its green color and was as white as Dorothy's dress." The Wizard tells them, "But my people have worn green glasses on their eyes so long that most of them think it really is an Emerald City." This finishes the Wizard's explanation of the City's origins. And so they discover the truth about the Not-So-Wonderful Wizard of Oz and his Not-So-Emerald City.

The Transformed Wizard

The Wizard tells them he was secretly delighted when they first showed up in the Emerald City and heard that Dorothy had killed the Wicked Witch of the East. He saw this as his chance to do away with the Wicked Witch of the West. She had driven him out of the land of the West and he lived in deadly fear of her. His great facade was partly to impress the wicked witches into thinking he actually was a great wizard. "When you came to me I was willing to promise anything if you would only do away with the other Witch; but now that you have melted her, I am ashamed to say that I cannot keep my promises."

This sends a panic into them, as they wonder how they are ever going to get what they came for. The Wizard admits that he is a very bad Wizard, but not necessarily a bad man, and proceeds to help them in a way he can. He begins to explain to the Scarecrow that it isn't brains that he needs but simply learning, which he has been getting all along. "Experience is the only thing that brings knowledge, and the longer you are on earth the more experience you are sure to get." The Scarecrow agrees to the truth of this, but says he would still like something to take with him. In the book, the Wizard gives him a token brain, filled with bran and a few pins and needles to prove he is sharp. In the film he presents him with a diploma, conferring upon him the honorary degree of Th.D.—Doctor of Thinkology. This satisfies the Scarecrow.

Turning to the Lion, the Wizard explains that he is merely confused about courage. "You are under the unfortunate delusion that simply because you run away from danger, you have no courage." There is a fine line between fear and wisdom, and one does not want to mistake the voice of wisdom for fear. Often what we think is fear is really our own prudence trying to get our attention. In the book the Wizard says, "There is no living thing that is not afraid when it faces danger. True courage is in facing danger when you are afraid, and that kind of courage you have in plenty. All you need is confidence in yourself." The Lion insists on something that will help him remember this. The Wizard goes to his cupboard and gives the Lion something to drink from a green bottle. This boosts the Lion's confidence. In the film, the Wizard pins a medal on the Lion and proclaims, "Therefore, for meritorious conduct, extraordinary valor, conspicuous bravery against wicked witches, I award you the Triple Cross. You are now a member of the Legion of Courage." This restores the Lion's dignity.

As for the Tin Man, the Wizard inquires if he is sure he really wants a heart. "It makes most people unhappy." "That is a matter of opinion," argues the Tin Man, "I will bear all the unhappiness without a murmur, if you will give me a heart." The Wizard suggests that he is fully capable of a heart's capacities, as proven by his dealings with the Wicked Witch. All he is missing is a testimonial. And so the Wizard makes another gesture of acknowledgment, presenting the Tin Man with a token heart and reminding him that a heart is not judged by how much a person loves, but by how much they are loved by others.

Despite his humbugness, the Not-So-Wonderful Wizard serves the situation, fulfilling a certain role. With his unmasking and subsequent confrontation, he too has become a newly transformed and empowered part of Dorothy. He has become the acknowledger of good deeds, affirming their good works with a positive voice. He provides the important component of encouragement, which in turn brings further empowerment.

And so the Wizard does not give anything to the soul parts other than tokens—reminders of what they have accomplished. He could not give them something they already had. He merely assigned them a task and affirmed their success when they completed it—the rest was up to them. Fulfilling their task fulfilled them, as it brought out the very thing for which they were looking. It activated what they thought they were lacking.

From Initiative to Initiation

What has taken place since the outset of the story could be considered an "initiation" experience for Dorothy—a modern form of initiation. *Initiation* is not a new idea. It is an idea common to virtually every culture throughout history. We may think of primitive societies with strange practices at sacred sites, where initiators test the courage, cleverness and passion of souls meeting rites of passage. But modern day clubs and institutions have their ways of initiation as well. However, an understanding of the essence of initiation has diminished in our modern times. It has slipped from its place of importance and is often turned into a misguided means of amusement, if it occurs as all. It has become a shadow of its former status.

Part of the problem is that even though initiation is not a new idea, it does need to be rethought and reinvented for our modern times. But what is meant by "initiation?" What is sought after by an initiation? Initiation refers to something that initiates or activates. To initiate literally means "to start something." We initiate a car's engine when we start it up. In the spiritual context, one purpose of initiation is to initiate or activate our soul capacities—our thinking, feeling and will—to get them going. We can trace how this happened with Dorothy as we look at her journey as an initiation experience.

In Kansas a certain set of circumstances surrounded Dorothy, setting the stage for her awakening. Pressure was mounting on the outside, while the outer supports were falling away. The door to her inner resources was opening. The way Dorothy responded to these circumstances indicated her budding ability for independent thinking, feeling and action. She made a personal declaration of independence when she ran away and then returned home.

When the scene shifted to Oz, we saw the result of her initiative reflected in the death of the Wicked Witch of the East, and the transfer of the Witch's magic slippers to Dorothy's feet. Endowed with new power, she then had to consciously use it. For this she needed to engage her thinking, feeling and will functions, which she embraced with her first steps along the Yellow Brick Road.

As Dorothy continued her journey, with her threefold soul at her side, she faced trials and tribulations—difficult challenges, as is the custom in initiation. She had no Aunt Em or Uncle Henry, no farm hands to turn to—that bridge was burned. It was a case of swim or sink, do or die. But this is what brought out the best in Dorothy and her soul parts. A potent challenge is usually inherent in an initiation, to catalyze real and lasting change. But nothing was insurmountable for them as they arose resourcefully to each occasion. Called into action, their activation took place.

It should also be noted that Dorothy was ripe for all of this to take place. In Kansas, she showed a strong connection to her longing for somewhere over the rainbow. The circumstances which unfolded there were but an answering to her deep yearning. They gave her the means to exercise initiative and prepare herself for the unfolding of her inner journey. This shows how, on one level, initiation is asked for, and not just something we are put through. Our initiative leads to our initiation.

The Poppy Field Initiation

The poppy field scenario can also be looked at as part of an initiation. One reason as to why the collapse in the poppy field occurred was mentioned earlier—its power of illusion. A second and different reason can be added here. The poppy field played an important part in the initiation process. It is helpful to understand the initial steps of an initiation in order to see how the poppy field was an integral part of Dorothy's.

In order for activation to take place, the soul parts first need to be made free from any constraints. To be able to function unimpeded, a break needs to be made with each other, and with the past. Dorothy's change of consciousness in the poppy field allowed such a break to take place. The soul parts became separated from each other and therefore the past patterns of thinking, feeling and action were broken. This temporary interruption opened the door for new ways to be forged further down the road.

From Imitation to Initiation

In the process of growing up our soul is in a way programmed through our imitation of things outside of us. Our thinking, feeling and will are developed in a particular way, as we imitate those around us. Our soul life is largely determined by our upbringing and the influences of our culture. But there comes a time when we need to free ourselves of this, and as an awakened self take control of our life, and how we think, feel and act. We need to be lifted out of a life of imitation by an initiation.

It is a necessary step in growing up that our soul be formed by our upbringing—this is what shapes and holds us together when we are too immature to be self-determined. But the relationship to our "preparents," the ones with the role of preparing us, is meant to be only a temporary one, and what they give us only a *preparation* for the work ahead of doing our own personal development. In order to be truly free we must to a certain extent undo what our upbringing has done for us and do the finishing work ourselves. The threads of the social fabric into which we have been woven have helped to hold us together, but ultimately become binding if not called into question.

What has been instilled in us may have supported us to a point, however, the supports of the past can become the constraints of the future if we don't bring consciousness to them. To a large degree, perhaps unknowingly, our thinking, feeling and willing has been done for us. Our soul life has been upheld by forces other than our own selfhood.

If we carry on in life without realizing why we do what we do, we cannot truly call ourselves free. Automatic responses need to be ceased or at least scrutinized, and ones of our own choosing put into place. This is not to say that we reject what we have learned from outer sources, but rather we take the responsibility to determine what influences us. In doing this we can ask ourselves questions such as—Are we self-determined or do we do things simply out of imitation and habit? Are we "self-made" or still purely products of our upbringing? How much do we determine for ourselves the way we think, feel and act and how much of it is determined by something or someone else? It is the mission of the self to undergo an initiation process that will answer these questions and reveal the direction in which further work needs to be done.

From Breakdowns to Breakthroughs

There is a step in initiation that temporarily interrupts the soul's usual flow. This is so there can be a reconstitution of the soul, a reconfiguration of its makeup. The thinking, feelings and will need to find a new relationship to each other and to the self. This may mean chaos for a time—a temporary loss of balance, as each soul part becomes free from the influences of the past and from the influences of each other. But this is a necessary stage. When it happens it simply indicates new ground for growth is being broken. The poppy field was exactly such an opportunity. It was the intermediate stage of initiation where the connection to the self was cut off and the past configuration of the soul broken. Things went out of balance as seen in the Scarecrow's (head) hysteria, the Tin Man's (heart) emotional outpouring and the Lion's (will) inertness.

This stage of inner development may be reflected outwardly in our lives. It may translate into a mental or emotional breakdown, a relationship breakup, the loss of a job, moving, a financial collapse, an identity crisis or a transition of some kind. It is sometimes referred to as "a dark night of the soul."

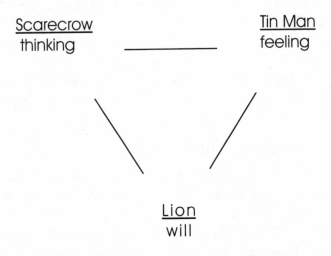

The Unintegrated Soul

The elements of initiation can appear in all manner of scenarios, large or small, in our day to day lives. In this way the whole world is now our sacred initiation site, and all of life our initiator. It is in the varied circumstances of life, and our response to them, that the path of modern initiation is walked. We all meet many rites of passage in our daily lives, perhaps of which we have little or no awareness. But everywhere lie opportunities for furthering our own initiation.

After a stage of chaos and imbalance occurs, the best is yet to come. Once the old ties are cut and former ways shed, a new and self-determined balance can be forged. The soul and self can be reunited in a new relationship. We only temporarily let go of the way things are, so we can get a new grip. If carried through with this positive view in mind, breakdowns can lead to major breakthroughs, and to new levels of being that would otherwise be missed. As Goethe pointed out, all division and separation occurs so that union of a higher kind can take place.

In Dorothy's case the poppy field appeared as a breakdown—and on one level it was. But it also became a breakthrough. When Dorothy regained consciousness, a stage of initiation or rite of passage had been passed and she was free to face the future with newness in every step.

Taking Up a Task to Forge New Forces

The next step of the initiation was the mission given by the Wizard. They found when they arrived at the Emerald City, it took more than just asking to get what they wanted. They had to do something for it themselves. As reluctant as they were at first, it presented the ideal opportunity to find and forge a new and self-determined balance. The old Dorothy and her former ways were left behind in the poppy field, and now her response to her future challenges would bring about new ways of thinking, feeling and acting. She could become a new being.

At first things appeared even worse than before, as the self became enslaved by the Witch, and the soul parts even more lost and scattered. But as they stayed with it, digging deeper into their resources, their determination was rewarded with unforeseen events assisting their efforts, until at last they successfully accomplished their task. Not only did they succeed in destroying the Wicked Witch for the Wizard, but a product of their efforts was that they came together in a new and free fashion, as the self and threefold soul. The initiation resulted in the ennobled abilities to think clearly, feel passionately and muster courage, all harmoniously under the auspices of the awakened self.

Dorothy and the Threefold Soul

From Naivete to Initiation

The idea of initiation should not be understood to mean we automatically become spiritual giants, or should even feel compelled to be so. There are stages and degrees to this extensive process, which is presented in an abbreviated form in this story. At its beginning stages, initiation simply involves removing the shrouds of *naivete* that keep us asleep and hold us back—even in our day to day dealings. Overcoming our naivete is the beginning of our spiritual awakening. It is the dawning of our *Transformational Day.*

What exactly is naivete? The word "naivete" comes from the Latin word "nativus," which means *a natural or unaffected state.* It is like an unhatched chick, still in its shell. The chick is in a natural state, unaffected by the influences of the world. Sheltered on the farm, Dorothy was in a natural state, not significantly affected by the influences of the world; in other words—*naive.* She had not yet broken out of her shell, stepping onto the road of life and getting in touch with the bigger picture.

Nothing can change until the shell of our naivete gets cracked and broken and we are set free of it. That is when life can really begin for us. Until then we are encased in the embryo of our upbringing. It is often a challenging or demanding situation that is called for to make the first crack in our shell. A challenge awakens us from our spiritual slumber—especially if we have not sought the awakening from within. Dorothy's difficult encounters along the way served this positive purpose. The wisdom of life is ever trying to guide us to higher levels of existence. Every breakdown is an opportunity for a breakthrough; every knock a boost. Our part is to recognize this and become a conscious partner in the process.

Initiation: Helpful or Harmful?

In the *Poppies* chapter, it was asked, "Poppies: Helpful or Harmful?" The answer is a paradox—they are both.

As representing drugs, it was said that they can be either helpful or harmful, depending on the intention and context of their use—*helpful* if for health-giving purposes, *harmful* if taken just for a "trip." The same thing can be said about initiation and the activation of our powers. It can be *helpful* if pursued with the right intention, *harmful* if done just for a "trip." The encounter with the poppies was potentially life-threatening, bringing about a breakdown of sorts. But with the Good Witch overseeing the process, it became a breakthrough and the dangers averted.

When the things we do to activate our powers are with the purpose of serving the greater good, and our intentions in line with life's intentions, then our initiation process is guided and guarded by higher powers. If our intention is otherwise, then the possibility of doing harm to ourselves and to others is everpresent. The breakdown part of initiation can leave us just that—broken down. But if we follow the path as presented to us by the wisdom of life, and do our best to proceed along those lines, then the next step can be made. Then we can forge new forces within ourselves, and enable ourselves to come fully into our power, as Dorothy did.

Had Dorothy not persevered on her journey and brought her initiation to a level of successful completion, the consequences would have been dire. The Wicked Witch of the West, who was using every bit of her own resources to thwart Dorothy's intention and disempower her, would have taken control of her inner world. If Dorothy had not followed through with her intention to destroy the Wicked Witch and fulfill her initiation, she would have been put under the merciless power of this manipulative part. The Witch would have become the puppeteer of Dorothy and her soul parts.

When an initiation is ill-conceived and goes awry, the final end is often a worse case than what it was before it began. But Dorothy held a sincere intention from the beginning. As a result, she was able to succeed, and the process brought no harm to her. Rather, she has helped herself immensely, as well as her soul parts, and will now be able to help others to a greater degree in the overall scheme of life.

What About Dorothy?

With the successful completion of the assigned mission, the Wizard has acknowledged the good works of the threefold soul with *rewards*, satisfying each of the soul parts that they have received what they came for. But while standing there, glowing with pride over their accomplishments, they suddenly realize someone has been left out. The Scarecrow points out to the Wizard that he has not given anything to Dorothy.

As for Dorothy, it is going to take more than a token of acknowledgment to get her back home. But a promise is a promise, and Dorothy has successfully completed her "homework." So the Wizard is forced into making a major decision. He says that the only way to get Dorothy back to Kansas is for him to take her there himself. And so preparations get under way to take Dorothy back home by balloon.

8

The Guidance of the Good Witch

With everything set to take Dorothy back home to Kansas—the hot air balloon ready, the Wizard calls all the people together to say goodbye before they depart. Dorothy is anxious to get going. But just when the Wizard is about to take flight, Toto pulls another one of his timely stunts, chasing a cat into the crowd. Dorothy follows after him. Suddenly the balloon begins to rise—the Wizard waving goodbye to everyone, including Dorothy. She tells him to come back—she wants to go too! But he shouts that he can't come back; he doesn't know how the balloon works! All eyes are "turned upward to where the Wizard was riding in the basket, rising every moment farther and farther into the sky. And that was the last any of them ever saw of Oz, the Wonderful Wizard."

Dorothy is left behind feeling more lost than ever. The others try to comfort her as she weeps. They assure her they are glad to have her stay with them. But the story doesn't end here. Things continue to unfold.

After some discussion, they decide to summon the Winged Monkeys again. They want to see if the monkeys can carry Dorothy over the great desert surrounding the Land of Oz to get her back home. Dorothy brightens up at this idea and gets the Golden Cap. After she speaks the incantation, the monkeys soon arrive. When she tells them her request, the Monkey King shakes his head and tells her that it can't be done. Her hopes dashed again, Dorothy cries at the disappointing response, as well as at wasting a wish.

Getting desperate for solutions, Dorothy asks the soldier with green whiskers for his advice, "Is there no one who can help me?" "Glinda might," he suggests, "The Witch of the South." When Dorothy asks how to get to her castle, he answers, "The road is straight to the South, but it is said to be full of many dangers to travelers." Despite possible further peril, they all agree there is no other option but to try. And so it is decided they will go together to seek the guidance of Glinda—the Good Witch of the South.

Away to the South

The next morning they start on their journey. This takes them through more interesting encounters. I will leave all but one of these adventures for the reader to explore. At one point they get stopped by a band of strange men known as Hammer-Heads. They are short and stout with big heads that are flat on the top and supported by thick necks full of wrinkles. A most peculiar trait is that they have no arms. They attack, as their name suggests, by shooting their heads out like hammers on their out-stretched necks, then recoiling them back after hitting their target. The Scarecrow takes a hit, which causes a chorus of boisterous laughter amongst this obviously obnoxious bunch. The Lion also takes a hit, leaving him bruised and sore.

They decide it is time to use the third and final charm of the Golden Cap. The Winged Monkeys arrive promptly and in time to rescue them from this attack. Dorothy asks the Monkey King if he can carry them to the country of the Quadlings in the South, where Glinda lives. "It shall be done," says the King. "At once the Winged Monkeys caught the four travelers and Toto up in their arms and flew away with them. As they passed over the hill, the Hammer-Heads yelled with vexation and shot their heads high in the air, but they could not reach the Winged Monkeys, who carried Dorothy and her comrades safely over the hill and set them down in the beautiful country of the Quadlings."

Finally, they make it to the South. Dorothy experiences more rich color here. Everything is red, in contrast to the yellow where the Winkies live, or the preference for blue in Munchkinland, or the green of the Emerald City. When they are escorted into Glinda's Castle they are introduced to a beautiful Witch who sits upon "a throne of rubies" and whose hair is of course, "a rich red color."

Glinda—The Witch of the South

After Dorothy tells Glinda the whole story of why they are there, Glinda says, "Bless your dear heart, I am sure I can tell you of a way to get back to Kansas. Your Silver

Shoes will carry you over the desert. If you had known their power you could have gone back to your Aunt Em the very first day you came to this country." The three others have something to say about this. "But then I should not have had my wonderful brains!" cries the Scarecrow, "I might have passed my whole life in the farmer's cornfield." "And I should not have had my lovely heart," says the Tin Man, "I might have stood and rusted in the forest till the end of the world." "And I should have lived a coward forever," declares the Lion, "and no beast in all the forest would have had a good word to say to me." Dorothy agrees with them and is glad they each got what they wanted. But now she is ready to get what she wants—to go home.

In the film, Glinda meets them at the Emerald City. When she tells Dorothy, "You don't need to be helped any longer. You've always had the power to go back to Kansas." the Scarecrow asks, "Then why didn't you tell her before?" To this Glinda answers, "Because she wouldn't have believed me. She had to learn it for herself." They all turn to Dorothy as the Tin Man asks, "What have you learned Dorothy?"

Then comes the climax of Dorothy's journey—the culmination of all the experience she has gained from it. She ponders for a moment then says, "I think that it wasn't enough to just want to see Uncle Henry and Auntie Em. And that if I ever go looking for my heart's desire again, I won't look any further than my own backyard, because if it isn't there, I never really lost it to begin with." Dorothy looks at Glinda and asks, "Is that right?" Glinda confirms with a nod, "That's all it is."

And so Dorothy has discovered that there is nothing she needs that she can't find, because everything she needs is already there. She realizes she's had what she's been looking for all along. She has realized her power within. Having this understanding Dorothy is told the magic slippers can now take her home in two seconds.

The focus again turns to the magic slippers. These shoes have repeatedly come up for attention since they first went on Dorothy's feet in Munchkinland. Now their meaning is no longer a mystery to Dorothy. The magic slippers symbolize the power that Dorothy began to activate in Kansas. The Witch of the *East* lost her clutch in the inner world as a result of Dorothy's initiative, and her shoes and power went to Dorothy. Destroying the Witch of the *West* took Dorothy to the other side of Oz and the rest of the road to conscious power. With that Dorothy can now fully use the power of the magic slippers to take herself home.

The symbol for Dorothy's power could really be anything—slippers, a broom, a magic cap, a magic carpet, a ring or any such mythical image. The symbol is secondary. What is shown as most important is the belief in one's own power and the instruction to use it. Dorothy has just finished stating her belief in her power. After she says her goodbyes to the others, Glinda now instructs her to use it. But before Dorothy makes that step, let us stop a moment and consider who this character Glinda is—the one giving the guidance to Dorothy.

The Good Witches

Who is Glinda the Good Witch of the South? What does she represent? In speaking of her we can also include the Good Witch of the North. The two *wicked witches*, the one of the east and the one of the west are related—sisters, as we learned earlier, and together make up one force. So too are the *good witches* related.

In the book, when Dorothy arrives in Munchkinland she meets a good witch who is introduced as the Good Witch of the North. In the movie she is referred to as "Glinda the Witch of the North." But in the book Glinda is really the Witch of the South, whom Dorothy doesn't meet until the end. The film writers lumped the two good witches together, which doesn't make much difference to the plot—one being from the north and the other from the south, they are two parts of the same axis—north and south. They are both benevolent and in a sense represent the same power—the Higher Power of Dorothy. The events of Dorothy's "Transformational Day" revolve around this north-south axis, as the earth does in its daily cycle. It is around the axis of the Higher Power that Dorothy's Transformational Day turns.

The Higher Power as the Pole Star

One could consider the Good Witch, as the Higher Power, and the words she spoke, "Follow the Yellow Brick Road," as the *Pole Star* or guiding point of Dorothy's journey. Astronomically, the Pole Star is the main reference point in the starry sky. It is the star that is in direct alignment to the earth's north-south axis. It has served sailors for centuries in navigating their ships over the seas. It serves land travelers as well, as a constant point of reference on the otherwise moving starry map.

As a steady point around which everything else revolves, the Pole Star acts as a reliable guide for navigation toward a destination. That is what the Higher Power's directive, "Follow the Yellow Brick Road," has been for Dorothy as she traveled toward her destination of home.

Those words were the one constant point to guide her, and an ordering factor in the otherwise swirling chaos.

The Good Witch as the Higher Self

With wand in hand the Good Witch has all the characteristics of a Fairy God Mother, as found in many fairy tales. She appears when needed with wise words and magic power, but otherwise remains behind the scenes to let the protagonist find the way. Thinking of Dorothy as the *essential self* in the array of characters, one could consider the Good Witch as the *Higher Self.* Other names may be preferred by some, such as the God Self, Divine Intelligence or Higher Consciousness.

The Higher Self, in the form of a Good Witch, appears at the beginning of Dorothy's inner journey and again at the end, but in fact oversees it every step in-between. Her presence is seen everywhere—she is *omnipresent* or all-present. She is dressed in a gown covered with stars and planets, holding a scepter-like wand, showing how she has the power of the cosmos in her hand—she is *omnipotent* or all-powerful. Her ornate crown sitting on her head, is a symbol not only of authority, but of authority based on knowledge, showing how she is *omniscient* or all-knowing.

In keeping with her position as the God Self, the Good Witch carries the symbol of the five-pointed star on top of her wand, which in ancient symbolism represented all to which a human aspires. She holds the final destination of the journey, the fulfillment of all human striving.

The Higher Self as the Pole Star for the Journey

A Question of Power

The Good Witch asked Dorothy a question when they first met in Munchkinland. It is an important part of the dialogue. "What the Munchkins want to know is—are you a good witch or a bad witch?" Dorothy responded innocently to this question, "I'm not a witch at all." Dorothy did not realize it, but she was really being probed about her use of power. She was being asked how she intended to use her newly activated power—what did she intend to become with it?

The answer to this question was apparently important to the Munchkins. They had been held in bondage for years by the power of the Wicked Witch of the East. Being set free of this, and Dorothy now possessing the power, quite naturally they wanted to know how she was going to use it. The Good Witch explained to Dorothy, "There are only four witches in all the Land of Oz, and two of them, those who live in the North and South, are good witches, those of the East and West, wicked witches." This means Dorothy, as the central character or self, holds the balance of power. She stands in the middle between good witches and bad witches, good and evil, and it is up to her which way things go. But the way Dorothy answered the question made it apparent she had not yet made any decision about how she would use her power. She didn't know anything about it yet. In the book she thinks to herself, "What could the little woman possibly mean by calling her a sorceress?"

Had Dorothy been conscious about what she had and how to use it, there would have been no need for a journey. But that was not the case. Dorothy's view of herself showed an abiding naivete. "Dorothy did not know what to say to this, for all the people seemed to think her a witch, and she knew very well she was only an ordinary little girl who had come by the chance of a cyclone into a strange land." Dorothy still considered herself "an innocent, harmless little girl, who had been carried by a cyclone many miles from home; and she had never killed anything in all her life."

And so Dorothy couldn't go home when she first arrived in Munchkinland. Even though, as Glinda said, "You've always had the power to go back to Kansas," until she realized it, she was stuck in Oz. Dorothy was the only one who could get herself home, but without an awareness of this something else had to take place—a journey.

A Journey for the Answer

Dorothy couldn't respond to the question, "Are you a good witch or a bad witch?" She lacked any sort of conviction one way or the other, and so how she would fare on the journey would be her response. Would she act wisely or foolishly? Would she follow the good or succumb to the evil? Would she use what she encountered in ways that would be helpful or harmful? What would be the moral basis from which she would use her power? Would she use her power for selfish or selfless purposes? Dorothy had to make a journey for the answer to the Witch's question.

As Dorothy was about to begin her journey, the Good Witch asked her if she had brought her broom. When Dorothy answered, "No," the Good Witch had no choice but to inform her that she would then have to walk. This second question put to Dorothy, asking her if she had brought her broom, is also a probing about power. A witch's broom is a symbol of power and this question a testing of Dorothy's conscious capacity to use it. But Dorothy replied she didn't have a broom—she was unconscious about her capacity for power. It is interesting how then, as part of the initiation mission given by the Wizard, *a witch's broom* is the very thing she is required to retrieve. The Wizard sent her in pursuit of a broom, or to discover more about her power.

A Quest for Conscious Power

It is also interesting how Dorothy had to walk to the Emerald City to get there the first time. Unconscious of her power, there was no other way. But to get back to the Emerald City, after being at the Wicked Witch's castle, it didn't matter how long or how far she walked—*walking* couldn't get her there. She had defeated the Witch and taken her broom. She was then going to have to use her power or not get back at all—which she eventually did using the Magic Cap. The journey to power is not only about overcoming our naivete of power, but also about overcoming our fear of using it once we have discovered it.

When Dorothy gets back to the Wizard, we find he is not as powerful as presumed. He tells them that the only reason he asked them to destroy the Wicked Witch of the West is because he couldn't do it himself. Dorothy destroyed the Wicked Witch of the East, and only she had the power to destroy the Wicked Witch of the West. Dorothy then proves to be her own most powerful resource in all the Land of Oz.

Activating Our Power

Dorothy's journey is symbolic of coming into power, of which Glinda informed her she had all the time. The irony is that Dorothy could have gone home right from the beginning had she known about her power. Instead she had to go through everything she did to find what was there all along. The power had to be realized and activated by Dorothy. We unleash what is in us when we go on a quest. Something is activated when we make an effort. And like the three soul parts said, they would not have received their own fulfillment had Dorothy not made her journey through Oz. They needed to be empowered too. And so the journey *was* and *wasn't* necessary.

9

The Witch and Wizard: The Faces of Duality

Dorothy's Shadow

Dorothy's journey home has involved a cast of characters. These characters could be referred to as the shadow aspects of Dorothy. They are called "shadows" because we don't usually see them as they are—in us. But rather we see just their *shadows* cast against the backdrop of our lives. They are a part of us, but become projected outwardly onto the people and events surrounding us.

In Dorothy's case, the parts she dealt with in Oz—the Scarecrow, Tin Man, Lion, Wicked Witch and Wizard initially cast their shadows outwardly onto those around her in Kansas—the three farm hands, Miss Gulch and Professor Marvel. The film cleverly captures this by using the same actors to play both the inner and outer roles.

The situations with the Kansas characters were an outer projection, or constellation of Dorothy's inner dynamics. They were the shadow or "telltale" of the state of her inner world. By making a conscious journey into her inner realm, to the source of the shadows, Dorothy was able to directly embrace and integrate these parts into her developing selfhood.

The shadow parts of us are not always dark as the term implies. They could just as likely be the unacknowledged light within us. In looking at the Witch and Wizard, they are such multilayered characters they could be viewed as either the unsavory side of human nature, or as the source of Dorothy's power. We will first look at them as portraits of evil.

The Wicked Witch and the Not-So-Wonderful Wizard

At face value the Witch is stereotypical, her evilness obvious from first glance. She is wicked enough to try to kill Dorothy. She wants to have the magic slippers and rule Oz. She exudes greed, jealousy, hate and other aspects of the nasty side of human nature.

The Wonderful Wizard of Oz, when we look more closely at him, is really the Not-So-Wonderful Wizard of Oz. He too has undesirable traits. But unlike the Wicked Witch's blatant brand of evil, he is more subtle in his ways—putting on the appearance of goodness. The Wizard and his glowing Emerald City illustrate the seductiveness of a wonderful but false image. Even the fact that the entire story is named after "The Wonderful Wizard of Oz" shows the ability to allure that this character has and to take the center even though he is by no means the central character. In reality the

Wizard is intimidating, cynical and pretentious. After Dorothy's discovery of his true identity, hidden behind his grandiosity, she began calling him the "Great and Terrible Humbug."

Combined, the Witch and Wizard's characteristics are a sampling of the egotistical or "ego" aspects of humanity, illustrating base behavior at its lowest. Each is power hungry and manipulative in their own way. The Witch is openly a controller, enslaving the Winkies in their own realm. The Wizard is cloaked in his control over the Emerald City—an opportunist taking advantage of others' ignorance. Pitted against each other, they are arrogant and insecure at the same time about their power.

Dorothy as the central character, or self, is challenged with overcoming this "evil" from both sides, or else being overcome by it. This challenge is a part of Dorothy's initiation, and a response to the Good Witch's question, "Are you a Good Witch or a bad witch?" Dorothy has to prove her resistance to evil. Life is full of temptation and none of us are exempt from the possibility of performing evil ourselves. How do we prevent these traits from manifesting in our own behavior?

The Dynamic Dualities

Evil is like a weed in our spiritual garden—it tells us something about our soil. Evil or ego arises as a result of imbalance. The antidote is to develop *balance* in our inner soil and let goodness flourish there, so bad seeds cannot take root. That is how the assault of evilness, as presented by the Witch and Wizard was foiled by Dorothy. Her journey was a quest for balance.

In speaking about balance it shifts us into looking at the Witch and Wizard in another way. To gain her balance Dorothy had to find it between the two sides, as represented by the Witch and Wizard. As important as these characters are in themselves, so too is the *dynamic* between them. In these two characters is seen the striving for balance between the dualities of life. They are best looked at together because they are actually two sides of the same coin. They are the faces of Dorothy's duality.

Dualities are everywhere. From our personal perspective we each experience left and right, front and back, above and below. From our earth perspective we experience day and night, which brings with it light and dark, hot and cold, expansion and contraction. There is also hard and soft, fast and slow, inward and outward to name but a few.

Dualities are what provide the conditions for life and growth—for creating *form* in the physical realm. The spiritual counterparts of the dualities are what provide the conditions for *spiritual* life and growth—to bring form to our selfhood.

The movement between the Witch and Wizard is what catalyzed the growth of Dorothy's selfhood. Her journey is a back and forth movement between the Wizard and the Witch or a back and forth between the dualities of life. Dorothy is first introduced to the Wicked Witch in Munchkinland. She then begins her journey to find the Wizard. Along the way she encounters the Wicked Witch again in the forest. This pushes her onward toward the Wizard. She again encounters the Witch by way of the poppy field. Finally, she makes it to the Emerald City and meets the Wizard. What does she then have to do? She must go and face the Wicked Witch. She deals with the Witch and then returns to the Wizard. Her journey is a back and forth movement between the Wizard and the Witch or the dualities of life.

This dynamic is shown well with the lemniscate, or infinity symbol found in ancient Egyptian symbolism.

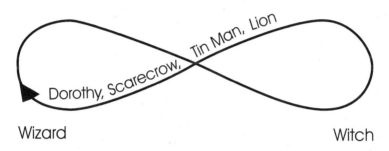

Wizard   Witch

The Back and Forth
Between the Wizard and the Witch

Dorothy's back and forth weaving between the Wizard and the Witch is key to her transformation. It is a weaving together into oneness the duality that runs through all life. The outer shadow of this dualism was first seen in the encounters with Miss Gulch and Professor Marvel. These encounters were an outer reflection of what was happening inwardly in Dorothy—the converging of the two sides within her.

The duality of *hot* and *cold* could be considered here. Miss Gulch was the bearer of cold and Professor Marvel the bearer of warmth. When hot and cold weather fronts meet, storms are a result. This is what causes tornados. The encounters with Miss Gulch and Professor Marvel, leading to Dorothy's meeting with the twister, was symbolic of the convergence of Dorothy's dualistic nature.

When Dorothy entered her inner realm she was then able to work directly with the spiritual duality of hot and cold, as personified by the Wizard and Witch, and directly harness these forces to bring her selfhood into form.

Life and *death* are another duality to consider. We encounter these more than just at the time of our birth and death. They are an ongoing dynamic in all growth processes. They are present in every process of becoming. The Witch is obviously the *bearer of death*, overshadowing Dorothy with its threat every step of the way. In contrast the Wizard elicits in her *hope of life*. Through the middle Dorothy follows a process that brings about growth. Looking at a few more of the dualities such as levity and gravity, light and darkness and masculine and feminine we can begin to understand the Wizard and Witch as metaphors of the dualistic agents helping Dorothy on her transformational journey.

Levity and Gravity

Levity and *gravity* are dualistic forces of nature, and are necessary to bring about balanced growth. Gravity helps us to keep our feet on the ground while levity helps us to grow upright. The same could be said of their effects on the spiritual level. Levity and gravity influence us as joy and sorrow, pleasure and pain, ecstasy and agony. Joy uplifts us or gives levity to our inner life. Sorrow brings us down keeping us rooted in reality. Both are needed to maintain inner balance. The ancient Greeks recognized this and employed these powers in their theater. The two masks of the Greek dramatic arts—one laughing and the other crying, represent comedy and tragedy—the artistic expressions of levity and gravity.

In Oz the Wizard is the levity side and the Witch represents gravity. The way they each exit the story shows this well. The Wizard lifts upward into the sky, while the Witch melts downward into the earth. The realm they each live in also reflect these qualities. The Wizard's Emerald City is light and uplifting whereas the Witch's domain is dark and depressing. The Witch is all too aware of her misery, telling Dorothy it is kind of her to visit her in her loneliness. The Wizard endeavors to live above his pain. The songs of the film even reflect these opposite extremes. The Winkies chant a somber O-E-O, O-EEE-O. In marked contrast the citizens of the Emerald City sing the day away with ha-ha-ha, ho-ho-ho and la-de-das in the "merry old Land of Oz."

The buoyancy or levity of the Wizard's realm shows a side that tries to be up all the time. If left unchecked however, it leads to an extreme state as seen in the attitudes of the people. They tell of getting up at twelve and starting work at one, taking an hour for lunch and then at two are done. But is that realistic? Life is not meant to be so "up and easy" all the time.

Dorothy met the shadow of these sides in her outer realm. She encountered levity through Professor Marvel, while Miss Gulch was the heavy. In her inner realm Dorothy met and mastered these two forces, working directly with them through the Witch and Wizard. As *inner* levity and gravity they provided the conditions for the balanced growth of her selfhood.

Sympathy and Antipathy: Opened and Closed

Dorothy's encounters with the Witch and Wizard illustrates two more important capacities for the development of our selfhood. That is the duality of *sympathy* and *antipathy*. In the most general sense sympathy means a moving toward something or an openness to it. The words *sympathy* and *symphony* come from the same root. If we want to be in "symphony" or harmony with something we open ourselves to it in "sympathy." We then resonate with it.

The opposite of sympathy is antipathy. It is a moving away from something or being closed to it. If we want to keep ourselves separate from something or resist its influence then we have antipathy to it. The duality of attraction and repulsion are akin to these.

Without a balance between these two capacities our relationship to the world may lean too much one way or the other. If we have too much sympathy or openness, we tend to lose ourselves in others. We lose our center and weaken our awareness of ourselves. On the other hand if we have too much antipathy, we become too closed off from others. We may become stuck in our own center or too "self-centered."

The middle ground between sympathy and antipathy is *empathy*. This third capacity is what emerges out of a mastering and blending of the other two. To have empathy toward a person is to be able to identify with them while maintaining who we are. It is the power to be open to others but not lose ourselves in them. With empathy we can build a bridge to another person's world while at the same time holding onto our own. With it we have a relationship to the world that is neither too open nor too closed.

In traveling the Yellow Brick Road Dorothy moved with openness and sympathy toward the Wizard. With the Witch she had antipathy in trying to avoid her. Out of the middle of these modes was born empathy. Dorothy learned to neither run from the Witch in a fear driven antipathy, nor be duped by the Wizard in a naive sympathy. Rather her growing power of empathy gave her the clarity to see others as they were, as well as to see who and what she really was. She found the middle ground, which became the solid ground upon which she could stand as a strong and centered self.

Masculine and Feminine

Another duality to consider is that of the *masculine* and *feminine* principles. These are seen in the Witch and Wizard, in that one is male and the other female. They could be considered as the untransformed, unintegrated inner masculine and feminine sides of Dorothy.

When referring to the masculine and feminine principles we are speaking of the two sides we all have, whether we are a male or a female. They are aspects which reside in everyone in some balance. Historically speaking, women have more often been the bearers of the feminine qualities, having a greater tendency as nurturers. Men have been the bearers of the masculine qualities, with a more accentuated conquering capacity. Both sexes manifested their qualities directly as an extension of their biological disposition. But these qualities are no longer restricted to a gender base. More and more, a mix and balance of these qualities are being consciously cultivated by men and women alike.

In some traditions the marriage of a man and a woman is considered the joining together of two halves of a whole. But more to the point, marriage is a metaphor of what we as individuals are striving to bring about within ourselves, as a marriage of the two halves of our own wholeness. One of the objects of the journey is to make a conscious union of these two sides, or an inner marriage. This is the underlying message of many fairy tales where a prince and princess undergo a transformative encounter, ascend to a royal realm and are joined in oneness to live "happily ever after."

A baby is often the result of such a union. Likewise the marriage of our masculine and feminine sides enables us to bring something new into existence. The self is born through such a union. As with raising a child, the growth of our selfhood is fostered by the integration of the influences from our male and female sides. This is what Dorothy achieved through her work with the Witch and Wizard. She transformed and married her inner masculine and feminine sides, blending their energies to bring about the development of her selfhood.

Light and Dark: The Rainbow Makers

The Wizard and Witch are also expressions of the qualities of *light* and *darkness*. The Wizard's glittering city is a realm of light, while the gloominess of the Witch's domain represents darkness. These polarities call into question the effects of light and darkness on the development of the self.

The day and night rhythm of the outer world means the earth spends part of its time in light and the other part in darkness. The result of this is not a world that is gray but rather one that is full of color. How is this explained?

The philosopher Goethe explained color as the interaction of light and darkness. This phenomenon is seen at both sunrise and sunset when the interaction between the light and darkness is at its most intense. Light penetrates the darkness at sunrise and darkness overcomes the light at sunset, both occurrences giving rise to colors in the sky.

Rainbows are also the result of the interaction of light and dark. Rainbows are not permanent fixtures in the sky but exist only for the time that light and dark meet. The sun's rays struggle to penetrate the obstruction of the rain and clouds. Color is the result of this dynamic.

In Dorothy's journey we are seeing the nature of light and darkness in a spiritual sense. It is a meeting of spiritual light and spiritual darkness. Dorothy began her encounter with light and darkness in the outer realm with Professor Marvel and Miss Gulch. In the inner realm she meets these aspects of herself in the Wizard and Witch.

Light is often associated with goodness and darkness with evil. Dorothy made this mistake initially in her naivete, running to the light of the Wizard and away from the darkness of the Witch. But as seen outwardly, light and darkness are both elements of nature and both are needed for growth. What the Witch provided for Dorothy's growth was just as much needed as what the Wizard provided. We are beings with both a light side and a dark side and both come into play in our inner work. As with *Beauty and the Beast*, neither side alone is complete. The two go hand in hand to bring about a metamorphosis into wholeness.

To get home Dorothy couldn't just hang out in the light of the Emerald City waiting for it to happen. Her light side, the Wizard, sent her into her dark side, the Witch. In the end this is what caused her to realize her power and to be able to take herself home. As C. G. Jung stated, we become enlightened not by dwelling on light but by making the darkness more conscious. We need to bring the light of consciousness into the dark, and the darkness of the unconscious into the light. We need to accept the role of both our light and dark sides in our personal development. It is the interaction of the two that creates color in our lives. It was what helped Dorothy to discover more than *somewhere over the rainbow,* for which she longed from the beginning, but to actually create a rainbow within. The inner struggle between light and darkness is what gave rise to Dorothy's true self, which in the end is her true colors.

Partners in Creation

We have seen how the Wizard and the Witch are the faces of the dynamic dualities of life: light and darkness, masculine and feminine, levity and gravity and so on. There are many more dualities one could consider: positive and negative, passive and active, masked and unmasked.

Each pair of dualities stands as a separate window through which we can view the Witch and Wizard. By looking at ourselves through these windows we can better understand what is taking place in our lives and become more conscious in working with these partners in creation. But a third aspect first needs to be introduced to allow this. This third part, explored in the following chapter, is what empowers us to consciously harness these partners in creation—the dualistic dynamics—on our path of personal development.

10

Secrets of the Spirit: From Duality to Individuality

Dorothy is a picture of the human condition. Her journey shows the challenge facing humanity to evolve. The future of evolution is calling for each of us to "individuate" or to become individuals. To be independent requires becoming an individual. But how exactly does this take place? What do we need to know to move forward in this? How can we best facilitate this goal? Some of the secret to this lies hidden in the word "individual."

The word "individual" is made up of three Latin words: "in," "divi" and "dual." It means "not divided in two." To be an individual means that we are *not divided in two*. It indicates that at one time we were divided in two but are no longer. Out of a dualistic nature *oneness* has been created.

Dorothy's dealings with the Witch and Wizard led to her becoming an individual, or "not divided in two." As explored in the previous chapter these two characters are more than antagonists in the plot. They are personifications of the dualities of life. By working with them as such Dorothy took her *dualistic* nature and turned it into a *oneness*. She became an individual.

The Creative Tension Between the Wizard and the Witch

The Witch and Wizard were arch enemies, rivaling for the upper hand in Oz. The conflict between them illustrates the tension that exists between opposites. This tension is clear in such opposites as attraction and repulsion, levity and gravity and life and death. Dorothy as the central character, or creative self, is the bearer of this tension.

On the level of our selfhood, the source of all stress and tension lies in our uncertainty about ourselves—our uncertain self-esteem. It is due to the unfinished business of building our selfhood. We have not yet reached the end of the Yellow Brick Road, completing our individuation. Our at times fragile and fluctuating self-esteem is a signal of this. The Good Witch's question to Dorothy, "Are you a good witch or a bad witch?" could be rephrased, "What are you going to become with your power Dorothy?" But Dorothy was only at the beginning of the conscious development of her selfhood when asked this. She had yet to walk the path of self-creation. And so she had to work with the tension of the opposites, the rivalry between the Wizard and Witch, to bring forth the answer.

Each one of us is a commissioned artist given the task of self-creation. This is the greatest artistic endeavor of all. As with all artists, there is a sense of tension as we face our unfinished creation. But the tension actually serves to heighten our creativity—until the creation is complete. The road to becoming an individual is a highly artistic path and one that requires a tolerance for this creative tension. When Dorothy finished her journey of self-creation, the Witch and Wizard were gone, as was the tension. The engaged consciousness of the self had turned duality into individuality.

Mother Earth and Father Sky

Physically one of the greatest creative acts is that which takes place between a male and a female resulting in the birth of a new human being. It is a metaphor for what can take place spiritually in each of us as we bring forth the birth and development of our selfhood.

The birthing of our selfhood involves the union of our inner male and female sides. When we engage and integrate our masculine and feminine qualities an inner marriage takes place, giving birth to our selfhood. This dynamic may remind one of the mythological image of *father sky* and *mother earth*. The creative energy of the cosmos meets and marries the fertile earth. An impregnation occurs resulting in the birth of a new sun. This might have been in the back of Baum's mind when he wrote *The Wizard of Oz*. With a Wizard who ascends into the sky and a Witch who descends into the earth, this ancient image appears to have influenced this modern tale.

From the moment of our birth we are influenced by masculine and feminine energies, each offering their distinct creative flavor. This usually begins with our "preparents," the ones who prepare us for the road ahead. They are our first contact with these forces and foster our growth as far as they can. But where our preparents can no longer help us, determines where our work begins. We are left with the legacy of their strengths, weaknesses and imbalances. It is then up to us to parent, or re-parent if you wish, ourselves by way of our inner parentage.

It is increasingly becoming our evolutionary task to do this *parenting work*—self-parenting or parenting of ourselves. It requires a connection with our personal parenting powers. Dorothy represents this emerging new model of the human being, where the *inner parents* and *inner child* all reside within one. Dorothy understood this at the end of her journey when she said she no longer needed to look any further than her own back-yard—or outside of herself. She realized everything is contained within. The journey just helps our consciousness to "catch up" with this reality.

Our Spiritual Parentage

We all begin life with dependency on those around us. We have no choice as a child. We receive parenting and we grow. But what causes us to grow and mature physically is more than just what our parents give us. It is also the nurturing or parenting forces of nature. The rhythm of night and day, darkness and light, causing us to sleep and awake, is an example of natures fathering and mothering. Gravity and levity are also at work, keeping our feet planted on the earth while lifting us into uprightness. Heating and cooling, hardening and softening, expanding and contracting and all the dualistic dynamics are participants in the parenting process.

Likewise the spiritual side of these dualistic forces, our *spiritual parentage,* play into our *inner growth* and *development.* They assist us to develop into upright spiritual beings. Dorothy, as an orphan, symbolizes how we are all spiritual orphans in search of the spiritual parenting of life. The dualistic forces of nature and our physical parents have brought us through the first stages of development. As spiritual orphans, it is up to us to engage our spiritual parentage to bring about the remainder of our growth—our spiritual development.

In preparation for this Dorothy had to cut the cord to her preparents—Auntie Em and Uncle Henry. She demonstrated this in running away from the farm to escape Miss Gulch, and in wanting to travel the road with Professor Marvel. Through these characters, as shadows of her spiritual parentage, Dorothy began the transference of the relationship from her preparents to her spiritual parents. When she entered her inner realm she then engaged directly with her spiritual parentage. The Witch and Wizard as representatives of the dualistic spiritual forces of life provided Dorothy with what she needed to grow and develop spiritually.

The aim of our development is to eventually be weaned off of our dependency on our outer parents through a growing relationship to our inner parents, and with consciousness to carry on for ourselves the processes of growth. As Dorothy encountered her spiritual parentage and moved toward her spiritual home she moved farther from her preparents and her childhood home. In the end when the Witch and Wizard were gone, Dorothy had received the inheritance of the powers of her spiritual parentage and had become an independent being.

Considered as parents, the Wizard and the Witch are of course odd looking. But this is true to life, because no parent is perfect. They are odd because they are at odds or at opposite extremes—out of balance in themselves. But there is a certain perfection in what they offer for growth.

The Wizard could be considered, in psychological terms, as the negative patriarch or *tyrannical father* and the Witch as the negative matriarch or *critical mother*. But notice, even as troublesome as they both were, it was not only by expulsion but also through integration that Dorothy dealt with them. Both were needed by Dorothy, *especially* in their out of balance ways. They gave her something to work with in finding her own balance. Just as *force* and *counter force* turn carbon into a diamond, and the contention between *darkness* and *light* produces the rainbow, Dorothy was able to take their opposite natures and bring them to a place of resolve and rest, creating something of value and beauty within herself. She found the balance point between the dualities—creating her individuality.

Matriarchy and Patriarchy: Overcoming Inner Anarchy

Until we take up the task of self-creation we for the most part experience our inner life as chaos—if we are aware of our inner life at all. This inner chaos could also be referred to as "inner anarchy." We all have inner anarchy to some degree.

In addressing our inner life as *anarchy*, it is helpful to know that the word "anarchy" comes from the Greek words, "an" and "archos," which means "without leader." *Anarchy* arises when there is a lack of leadership. *Inner anarchy* arises when there is a lack of inner leadership. Interestingly the words "patriarchy" and "matriarchy," with the shared root "archos," indicate leadership from the male and female sides.

History shows a back and forth shifting between patriarchal or male oriented leadership and matriarchal or female oriented leadership. The succession of kings and queens giving alternating rule is an example of this. As Dorothy's inner matriarch and inner patriarch, the Witch and Wizard, each in their own way vied for rulership over of the Land of Oz. It was finally Dorothy who determined the leadership, overcoming anarchy and bringing about a balance of matriarchy and patriarchy within herself.

After Dorothy threw the bucket of water at the Wicked Witch the Witch screamed, "In a few minutes I shall be all melted, and you will have my castle to yourself." Dorothy gained leadership in her inner land. The Winkies bowed on their knees and shouted, "Hail Dorothy." They recognized her rightful rulership of this realm. The Witch's broom, symbolizing power, was then passed to her—the newly enthroned self. Likewise before the Wizard disappeared, his rulership was turned over to one of Dorothy's soul parts. Through the integration of her inner Witch and Wizard, Dorothy blended the patriarchal and matriarchal sides of herself into a unified and balanced inner leadership. The critical voice of the negative matriarch became empowerment for Dorothy and the tyrannical patriarch became a positive voice within her. Dorothy mastered and transformed each side and became ruler of her inner realm.

Breaking Out of the Infinite Holding Pattern: Following the Middle Road

What led Dorothy to the mastering of her inner realm? Guidance is needed for such a *crowning achievement* to take place. The infinity symbol of the diagram illustrates how the dualities of life are in an endless dynamic. We can become caught infinitely between the influences of the Wizard and Witch, as each tries to dominate over the other. We will remain this way until we find a way to master them and break out of *the infinite holding pattern.*

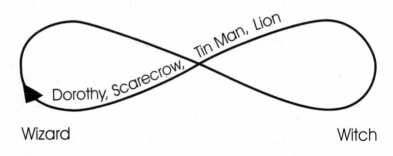

Wizard   Witch

The Back and Forth Between the Wizard and the Witch

Into the twosome of the Witch and Wizard, there needs to be invited a third spiritual influence—the Higher Self.

The Higher Self is wise, benevolent and deeply invested in our development. The Higher Self wants us to get home and knows the way. Breaking out of the infinite holding pattern of life begins when we make it our *intention* to move forward and have the *willingness* to

be guided in doing so. Dorothy fulfilled these require-
ments. She had the intention to move forward in her
life—she was longing for somewhere over the rainbow.
When the Higher Power told her to "follow the Yellow
Brick Road," she accepted the guidance willingly.

As Dorothy moved out on the road, her intention and
willingness made it so that all she encountered took her
closer to her "home goal." The back and forth between
the Witch and Wizard moved her forward, rather than
digging her into a rut, the way it had for Aunt Em and
Uncle Henry in their gray and dusty lives. Dorothy found
and followed the middle road which moved her beyond
the Witch and Wizard's endless influences. She broke
out of the infinite holding pattern.

When we move out with the same intention and
willingness as Dorothy, we too will move beyond the
infinite holding pattern. Life becomes something with
a destination, instead of just a series of meaningless
meetings. Outer circumstances are synchronistic with
inner developments. Life then becomes a highway to
home, and every occurrence the brick and mortar of
self-creation.

The Higher Power: Between Both and Above All

In following the Yellow Brick Road, it meant Dorothy
was following the ongoing guidance of her Higher
Self—her Pole Star. In doing this she was lead on the
middle path, through the Land of Extremes, to a new
place of inner balance and poise. The Higher Power
became the organizing factor in the chaos, helping her
to get all her parts in the right place. The Higher Self's
words provided direction where there was anarchy and
guided Dorothy to turn the artistic tension of duality

into individuality. Dorothy could not have done it without the help of her Higher Self. The Higher Self helps us in orchestrating the influences of life to create the masterpiece of our own selfhood. Life in the broadest sense, with all the dualistic dynamics, becomes our spiritual parentage.

Even though the Good Witch remained in the background, as compared with the Wicked Witch and the Not-So-Wonderful Wizard, she stood *between both and above all.* The Higher Power being between the dualistic extremes, helps us draw from both sides what we need, as artists of our inner being. We are guided with the array of influences on life's palette in our self-artistry. We are helped in choosing from things that warm us, things that cool us; things that raise us, things that lower us; things that harden us, things that soften us; things that expand us, things that contract us—whatever is needed at each step of our growth.

The Higher Self leads us through the highs and lows of life to create a balanced self. The levity and gravity of surrounding circumstances are mediated to help us grow into upright spiritual beings, being neither overconfident nor underconfident. Out of our sympathies and antipathies we develop empathy and true compassion. Empathy becomes the vessel or container in which the self can work in the world.

We are lead to be hard when we need to be hard and soft when we need to be soft, and to find the balance between malleability and permanence. With this the self can be brought into form.

The intervention of the Higher Power helps turn black and white situations into consciousness expanding ones, where two options are turned into a spectrum of possibilities. Our soul is also developed by this, gaining even greater refinement in the process. Our thinking finds more perspectives. In our feelings we find more nuances. And the set of the sail for our will's intentions can develop more gradations.

It is not just a matter of transcending the opposites, but of creating something out of them. It is only with the assistance of the Higher Self that we can reconcile the different sides of ourselves to bring about the development of our selfhood—and with the development of the self—the capacity for consciousness. As with Dorothy, we are lead to a place of *higher self realization*.

The Weaving Between Wizard And Witch
To Higher Self Realization

The Apex of Understanding

As Dorothy made her journey through Oz, she overcame whatever obstacles arose before her. In all that she overcame, she overcame the greatest obstacle of all—ignorance. She especially overcame ignorance about herself, as the Yellow Brick Road unfolded as the journey to "self-knowledge."

What is the essence of the understanding Dorothy received? What is it that she learned about herself during her journey? Firstly, when the Tin Man asked her, "What have you learned Dorothy?" she told them, "It wasn't enough just to want to see Uncle Henry and Auntie Em." Dorothy had thought what she wanted most was to be back with her family in Kansas. But by the end she realized that wasn't enough. There was more to life than being on the farm with family. Wanting to be on the farm with family was fine, but a whole other world had revealed itself to her. She realized she had an inner world as well. She then realized it was just as important to have an inner life as an outer one.

Dorothy continued with more about her learning. "And that if I ever go looking for my heart's desire again, I won't look any further than my own backyard, because if it isn't there, I never lost it to begin with." We could rephrase Dorothy's revelation to, "I know who I am, and I know what I have!"

Dorothy made it to *the apex of understanding*. She reached the pinnacle of truth. She realized she had everything she needed within her. She could now look to herself for answers. It took a long journey to reach that realization, but to use two clichés, she had *climbed the highest mountain* and *touched the farthest star*.

The "apex of understanding" is the highest point of understanding one can reach. It is the highest point of knowledge one can attain. It is the conjunction point where the dualities meet, and the balance point where the self becomes fully realized. Dorothy's journey to "higher self realization" brought her to this point of understanding.

Dorothy and the Dynamics of Spirit

When Dorothy met the Good Witch in Munchkin-land, she didn't recognize it at the time, but what she was looking for stood right before her, the higher consciousness of the Higher Self—enlightened understanding. The Good Witch knew what Dorothy was needing to know—that she already had what she was looking for—but couldn't tell her. Instead she sent her on a journey of learning, or put her in a process, so she could learn it for herself. The God Self has that kind of wisdom. It knows what the lower self needs to know, yet leaves it free to find it for itself.

Even when the Good Witch made the probing question about power to Dorothy, "Are you a good witch or a bad witch?" she didn't need to hear the response as much as Dorothy needed to hear the question. The Good Witch already had perfect understanding of the situation. But in her wisdom she went along with where Dorothy was in *her* understanding—so Dorothy was left free to find the answer her own way. And so the Good Witch continued with the dialogue, asking if Toto was the witch. Dorothy again answered with innocence, still not understanding the point of the question. The Good Witch finally exclaimed, "Well, I'm a little muddled. The Munchkins called me because a new witch has just dropped a house on the Wicked Witch of the East, and there's the house, and here you are." Actually Dorothy was the one who was a "little muddled." She did not recognize what had taken place in her life. In the book she is called a "noble sorceress" and honored as one endowed with great power—which is precisely right. That is what she had become. The problem was that everyone else could see it, except Dorothy. The missing component was Dorothy's consciousness. It needed to do some "catch-up" work.

And so in her wisdom the Good Witch knew Dorothy needed to *muddle* her way along the Yellow Brick Road to enlightened consciousness, as we all do, to some degree. She could see Dorothy needed to go on a long walk, with her new shoes, to discover the key to her power—greater awareness about herself. So she sent Dorothy in search of the Wizard, knowing all along what the Wizard was like and that he couldn't take Dorothy home, and also knowing what the Wicked Witch would try to do. She sent her anyway, because she knew it would give her what she needed as leverage for her consciousness raising, and to realize the truth about herself.

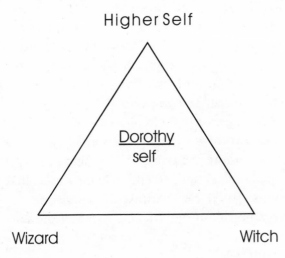

The Dynamics of Spirit

Dorothy succeeded in dealing with these characters, the Witch and the Wizard. Out of these two aspects, under the guidance of the third—the Higher Power, emerged the newly formed and empowered self. As with the *threefold soul,* in the center of this *threefold spiritual dynamic* stands Dorothy as the developing self.

The Initiated Self

As partners on the journey, the soul parts helped Dorothy in the climb to the apex of under-standing—each contributing what they could to her enlightenment. When Dorothy shared what she had learned, the Scarecrow said, "But that's so easy! I should have thought of it for you!" The Tin Man said, "I should have felt it in my heart!" But Glinda said, "No—she had to learn it for herself."

The Scarecrow could have had the thought. And the Tin Man could have had the feeling. And the Lion could even have had the right intention. But that alone is not enough. Our soul capacities of thinking, feeling and will help us in coming to a higher understanding—being the instruments of cognition or knowing, but it ultimately has to become the experience of our core—the self.

The self has to become initiated or active in higher understanding to the degree that it can live its power. This is the point to which the Good Witch has guided Dorothy. Dorothy has arrived there. She has articulated her new found understanding of herself and her power. She realizes it, now she can use it. She can at last go home.

11

There's No Place Like Home

At the close of Dorothy's time in Oz, the soul parts each go to a place where their newly discovered powers can be put to work. The Scarecrow with his brains becomes the ruler of the Emerald City; the Tin Man with his fondness for the Winkies becomes their ruler; and the Lion with his newly discovered courage becomes the King of the Beasts in the Quadling forest. Each soul part finds a place to call home in Dorothy's inner world as she returns back to her outer.

Now that Dorothy realizes her power she can finally use her magic slippers. Glinda tells her, "The Silver Shoes have wonderful powers. And one of the most curious things about them is that they can carry you to any place in the world in three steps, and each step will be made in the wink of an eye. All you have to do is knock the heels together three times and command the shoes to carry you wherever you wish to go." Dorothy commands that they take her to Aunt Em and Uncle Henry. In the film Glinda tells Dorothy to close her eyes and repeat, "There's no place like home...There's no place like home...There's no place like home..."

Dorothy's Paradigm Shift

The words, "There's no place like home," heard at the end of the film actually appear much earlier in the book. Dorothy first says these words while telling the Scarecrow about Kansas. These words have been spoken by many, long before *The Wizard of Oz* made them famous. Centuries ago the poet Novalis asked, "Where are we really going?" then answered his own question, "Always home!" The idea of "home" inevitably emerges as the ultimate ideal. But what and where is home?

This has been Dorothy's question from the beginning. It was implied in her orphanhood, then voiced when she became lost in Oz. At the beginning of her journey, *home* meant being back on the farm in Kansas. But by the time she reached the apex of understanding she realized, "It wasn't enough just to want to see Uncle Henry and Auntie Em." She starts out with one idea of home but by the end of her journey has another. Dorothy experienced a paradigm shift.

Dorothy does not say, "There's no place like Kansas!" She says, "There's no place like home." We know she commands the power of the magic slippers to take her back to Kansas but with her consciousness enlightened and her idea of home expanded what is she really meaning?

In growing up we develop an image of what home looks like to us. That would hold true for Dorothy. But as a result of her inner journey her sense of home now includes something else—something that extends beyond her home in Kansas. Part of the process of our journey is the *re-visioning* of our image of home—matching our impulse for home with new images of home. In Dorothy's paradigm shift her *impulse* for home is now matched with a new *image* of home.

Home as an Image

Describing with words what Dorothy possibly means by, "There's no place like home" is almost impossible. This statement points to something that can hardly be articulated. Because both book and film act only as mediums of the message, they each have their limitations as to how much of Dorothy's paradigm shift and new understanding they can convey. What is needed is for each of us to become active in our imaginations, to fill in for ourselves what may be the message of the story.

Using our *imagination* involves using *images*. Symbolic images have been used for centuries to convey spiritual ideas such as with the circle.

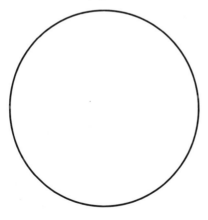

The All Encompassing Circle

The circle has been used since ancient times to describe what life looked like in its beginnings, in a unified state—a state of wholeness or togetherness. The circle was thought to describe symbolically what life looked like in its origins before division and diversification entered the picture. Put your finger on the page and trace the form of the circle. There is no beginning and no end—just a continuum. Life was an eternal and all-encompassing circle.

Two Worlds Wanting To Be One

While in Kansas Dorothy's experience of life was anything but a circle. Her experience was not one of oneness or wholeness. She expressed a yearning for something else, somewhere else. While in her "backyard" she pondered, "Someplace where there isn't any trouble? Do you suppose there is such a place Toto? There must be. It's not a place you can get to by boat or by train. It's far, far away...beyond the moon...beyond the rain." She was experiencing the tension between the two worlds. Dorothy then sang about somewhere over the rainbow. It was a longing to be connected to the other side. But when she arrived on the other side she then wanted to return—because she also longed to be connected with this side.

Dorothy's dilemma was that she could not be satisfied by either side alone. She was trapped by the longing of life—for there to be a healing of the split between the two worlds, a return to oneness or "the all-encompassing circle." What she was experiencing at the beginning would not be symbolized as a circle but rather as an infinity symbol, an infinite back and forth between two sides. This symbol was used before to show the back and forth between the Witch and Wizard, but it also fits to symbolize the back and forth between the outer and inner worlds.

Outer and Inner Realms

If one were to take a circle, made out of wire for example, and make a twist in it so that it crossed in the middle, the infinity symbol would appear. The circle would have changed form and produced another image. All that was contained in the circle is still there, but it has taken on a new shape. It still encompasses all that was in the all-encompassing circle, but now the oneness of the circle is split into two. Again put your finger on the page and trace the new form. It is a continuum, as is the circle, but is now broken into two halves.

This new form represents how we all currently experience the big picture of life—in bite sizes, as two separate worlds. We each have a Kansas state of mind and an inner Land of Oz—or a conscious part and an unconscious part. We go back and forth between the two. Sometimes we are on one side and at other times on the other. The outer and inner worlds are experienced separately—the *outer* by day or while conscious, and the *inner* by night or while unconscious—of which our dreams give us glimmers. Even though the two realms are one and the same, or two sides of the same coin, our experience of them is split, and so they appear as distinct and separate, as they did for Dorothy.

This splitting of our time between the two realms is seen in our switching back and forth between waking and sleeping consciousness. Notice that as you traced your finger on the form it could go only so far in each direction—on each side of the infinity symbol. Then it had to turn back, cross the crossing point or threshold, and return to the other side. Likewise we can be only so long in one world, then we need to return to the other. This is seen in how we can go only so long without sleep. Eventually we loose consciousness to this world, not only because our physical nature demands rest from this world, but also because our spiritual nature requires nourishment from the other. Then after a time in the "sleep world," we return to this one, because our growth also requires earthly experience. As with Dorothy, neither side alone can totally satisfy what we need to grow and be whole beings.

What Dorothy was really longing for was *the best of both worlds*—somewhere over the rainbow and this world at the same time. The tension between the two worlds was calling her to bring them back together in her experience. The development of our *individuality* means we also need to work with this *duality* of the outer and inner worlds. Within each of us is the potential to bring about a marriage of the inner and outer worlds, to achieve a simultaneous experience of them again.

When these two sides of our existence are brought back into oneness and the tension between them resolved, what might it look like symbolically?

Coming Full Circle

The idea of going over the rainbow, to "the other side" in search of a pot of gold or some such treasure, is a theme common to many fanciful tales. It is interesting to note that rainbows are actually circular. Usually depicted as arcs, rainbows are really circles when observed in their entirety. It is only from our limited earthbound perspective that they appear as arcs. We see half of a rainbow in the sky while the other half is out of our view, beneath the horizon. Their circular form is at times observable while flying. This phenomenon is a good analogy for how our limited earthbound perspective sees only half of what is going on in life. What goes on in the other half is hidden beneath the horizon of our consciousness.

When Dorothy finished her journey to the other side of the rainbow she stated, "It wasn't enough just to want to see Uncle Henry and Auntie Em." She realized there is more to life than what was goes on in her outer world. She understood that an inner life is as important as an outer one and that the two need to go together. By opening her consciousness to include the other half of life, making that which was unconscious conscious, she was able to embrace both sides of the big picture.

By following the Yellow Brick Road over the rainbow and back, it brought Dorothy "full circle," back to herself. She found herself standing at the center of her own *rainbow circle*. Dorothy refashioned the infinity symbol, with its infinite back and forth between two worlds, into an all-encompassing circle again. Such as with a wedding band, the circle represents a marriage into oneness.

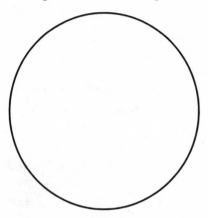

Coming Full Circle:
Outer and Inner as One

This is the challenge facing all of us on the modern path of initiation, that we become mindful of both sides at the same time, holding both in consciousness simultaneously. By doing this our experience of life will also no longer look like an infinity symbol, with two apparently distinct sides. Rather it will be an all-encompassing circle once again. And when accomplished, like Dorothy we will realize, "If I can't find it in my own backyard, it was never lost to begin with." We will discover everything we are looking for is within our own circle of being.

The Integration of Soul and Spirit

We have seen how the Scarecrow, Tin Man and Lion as thinking, feeling and will make up Dorothy's three-fold *soul*—symbolized with a triangle. The Wicked Witch, the Wizard and the Good Witch make up her threefold *spiritual* dynamic—also symbolized with a triangle. Placed together these geometric shapes represent Dorothy's total soul and spirit makeup.

All of these aspects of Dorothy were engaged with each other during the course of her journey. The Scarecrow, Tin Man and Lion—as the capacities of soul, had an affect on the Witch and Wizard; and the spiritual dynamics of the Witch and Wizard—as the content of soul, likewise on them. An example of this is seen in the dualism of *division* and *unification*. The Wicked Witch worked to *divide* the soul parts, whereas the Wizard's assigned task served to *unite* them. This duality affected the soul forces, dividing and uniting them at different points in the journey, fulfilling the purpose of forging them in a new way. All of this took place under the guidance of the third spiritual component, the Good Witch or Higher Self. This interaction between the three soul parts and the three spiritual dynamics illustrates the *integration* of Dorothy's soul and spirit natures.

In representing the integration of soul and spirit as two inter-connecting triangles, another image emerges—a six-pointed star. The six-pointed star is another geometric shape, also considered a sacred symbol. Today it is largely associated with Jewish symbolism, known as the "Star of David" or "Shield of David." But its use in Judaism began only around the Middle Ages. It was considered a significant geometric shape or sacred symbol prior to that in other cultures. It has been said to represent the union of heaven and earth or spirit and matter. It is a universally recognized image of union or integration.

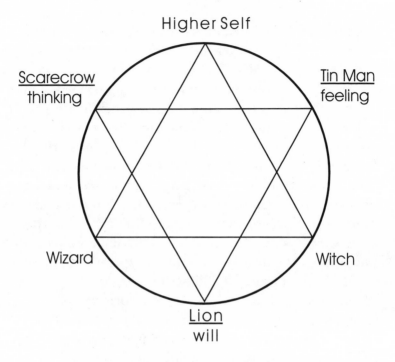

Higher Self

Scarecrow
thinking

Tin Man
feeling

Wizard

Witch

Lion
will

The Integration of Soul and Spirit

The Spiral: Turning Chaos into Creativity

Despite the fact that Dorothy had everything she was looking for all along, her story shows how she still needed to go through a journey to realize it. She had to go through a period of chaos and confusion. The *spiral* symbolized this throughout the story, starting with the spiraling tornado, then the spiraling Yellow Brick Road, then appearing again at the end as Dorothy is transported back to Kansas.

The spiral reminds us that the creative process is not a simple straight line. Creativity never goes in the same direction for long and at times has the sense of being chaotic. But "chaos" is simply the name we use to describe a creative order we don't fully understand yet. Uncertainty is part of the order of things.

Chaos is turned into *creativity* when we turn with it as such. It is then that the creative potential appears. If we take time to appreciate so-called chaos and work with it rather than resist it, it will become the very force we are looking for to take us where we want to go.

The Spiral: From Chaos to Creativity

Trace the spiral with your finger. It seems like you are going in circles—and you are. But as you do you pass through each of the six characters that contributed to Dorothy's growth. For a while you go in the direction of one, looking like you might arrive there. But as you continue you discover your direction changing and your finger moving toward another. Life is like that. Just when you think you know where you are going and have almost arrived—things change and you find yourself moving toward something else. It keeps us in the creative flow.

We can't get too settled when we are on the road of self-creation. For example, perhaps you like being on the Wizard's side—it gives you good feelings and so your Tin Man just wants to hang out in an Emerald City with all its wonderful illusions. Or perhaps you favor brain games and so you just want to be with your Scarecrow all the time. Except your Lion objects to this because he doesn't get the action he needs to stay in shape. Or perhaps you don't like involvement in life much at all and simply would rather just spend all your time communing with your Higher Self. But getting stuck in any of these parts of the six-pointed star would hinder our journey and our balanced self-development.

An interesting thing about the form of the spiral is that it implies motion. It draws our eyes into moving. In order for balanced growth to take place there must be movement. And so staying in one spot does not work. We have to keep spiraling along the Yellow Brick Road, letting all aspects of our being come into play. There is little one can do about this characteristic of life except learn to let go and work with whatever comes along next—realizing we are more than "human beings," we are also "human becomings."

Sometimes the creative process requires a lot of letting go—so that we be fully open to the cycles of creativity. But letting go should not be a problem when we understand that as we follow the course of the spiral we keep revolving around to the same archetypes, which allows us to get a new hold in a new way.

Often it is only our own uninstructed and unpartici-pating consciousness that blocks the best things from happening to us. But by working with the *creative chaos* or *chaotic creativity* of life, in the end we lay hold upon the greatest thing we could possibly want—our *self.* Like Parsifal, knight of the Round Table questing for the Holy Grail, in the end we discover the greatest treasure is what we become in the process. We discover the "Dorothy in us."

Out of Many—One

When Dorothy was held captive by the Wicked Witch, the Lion while mustering his courage said, "All right, I'll go in there for Dorothy." He did it for Dorothy. In the end everything was done for Dorothy, that she should become a new being of power and consciousness. Like a newly forming star, out of a swirling chaos, emerged the seventh part of the human puzzle, the center piece and purpose of it all—the empowered self. The other six parts all helped in the shaping of the seventh. It was the ultimate aim of all the interaction.

The Wizard made an appropriate comment when he decided he would take Dorothy back home. He referred to their destination as the land of "E Pluribus Unum." This is Latin for "Out of Many—One." This is the motto found on the seal of the *United States,* but ironically points to what we can achieve on a personal level as a *united state,* when all our parts are engaged in the devel-opment of our individuality—out of many, one.

The use of this motto in *The Wizard of Oz* is not a plug for the "good old U.S.A." as some suggest is the intent of the entire story. Rather it shows how America is built upon an important principle that is as applicable on a personal level as it is on a political one—that it takes many parts to build oneness. Out of many parts Dorothy's oneness was created. Dorothy's quest for home was a quest for wholeness.

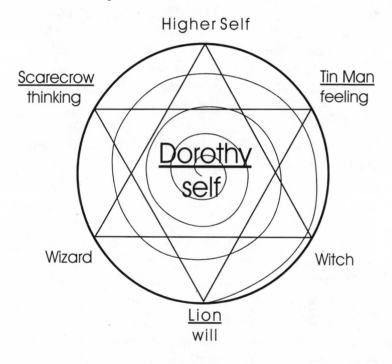

Higher Self

Scarecrow
thinking

Tin Man
feeling

Dorothy
self

Wizard

Witch

Lion
will

Out of Many - One

A Mandala

Throughout the course of this book a number of geometric symbols have lent themselves for diagrammatic description of the ideas being discussed. In joining all the shapes together a *mandala* has been formed, as seen on the front cover of this book. Mandalas have been used throughout the ages to house ideas that could not be communicated otherwise. Here one has emerged to show symbolically Dorothy's journey home.

The Answer

Several *questions* have been a part of Dorothy's journey. When she arrived in Oz she was asked by the Good Witch, "Are you a good witch or a bad witch?" or in other words, "What will you become with your power?" In return Dorothy had a question for the Good Witch, "Where is home and how do I get there?" All these questions add up to the same thing, for which Dorothy had to make a journey to find the answer.

Along the way Dorothy met a stork who asked, "Who are you and where are you going?" These questions again amount to the same thing. Who you are depends on where you are going. You become what you set your sights on.

With the ending of Dorothy's inner journey all the questions are resolved. Dorothy has found all the answers. What Dorothy sought for is what she has become. What she has become is now her home. "There's no place like home...There's no place like home...There's no place like home..."

12

The Dorothy in You

As Dorothy arrives back in Kansas, that is the end of her magic slippers. "Dorothy stood up and found she was in her stocking feet. For the Silver Shoes had fallen off in her flight through the air and were lost forever in the desert." Baum never intended to write a sequel. Dorothy's journey was complete and so the shoes were not going to be needed again. (It was public pressure in fact that led Baum to write thirteen more *Oz* books).

Home Again

After being whirled through the air Dorothy finds herself looking at the flat Kansas prairie again. "Before her was the new farm house Uncle Henry built after the cyclone had carried away the old one." The final chapter entitled "Home Again," is very short—seven sentences. "Aunt Em had just come out of the house to water the cabbages when she looked up and saw Dorothy running toward her. 'My darling child!' she cried, folding the little girl in her arms and covering her face with kisses.

'Where in the world did you come from?' 'From the Land of Oz,' said Dorothy gravely. 'And here is Toto, too. And oh, Aunt Em! I'm so glad to be home again!'"

In the book Dorothy's journey is framed as an actual time away in another land. The journey begins in a place in this world with which we are familiar—Kansas. It then takes her to another place of fairy tale dimensions, but brings her back to people wondering where she has been. In the meantime, a new house has been built to replace the one the tornado took away. Most fairy tales are not framed this way. Usually they are exclusively about an adventure in another land, with little reference to present day reality. But Baum's approach takes the fairy tale a step away from being pure fantasy, connecting it with outer reality, to underscore the validity of both worlds and the connection between them.

The film uses a somewhat different angle. As Dorothy repeats, "There's no place like home," we see a house spiraling through the air. Next we see Dorothy in bed, with Aunt Em by her side. The film turns back to black and white as Dorothy finds herself surrounded by grayness again. Dorothy begins to tell everyone about the place she has been. Auntie Em interrupts with, "You just had a bad dream." The film introduces the idea of Dorothy's journey being a dream. The two different endings add up to one question. Was Dorothy's experience real? Dorothy is convinced her experience was real.

There is no doubt Dorothy's new found belief in the other dimension is going to be challenged by the flat attitudes surrounding her. Uncle Henry attributes it to a bump on the head and Auntie Em keeps on about it being just a silly dream. But Dorothy insists, "It wasn't a dream. It was a place Aunt Em. This was a real truly live place. And I remember that some of it wasn't very nice—but most of it was beautiful! Doesn't anybody believe me?" Uncle Henry assures her that they do. But does he really mean that? Or is he just saying it to appease her?

The ending raises some issues. Is there another side of life that can be experienced consciously? Is there another world or is what we see all there is? Did Dorothy really go somewhere or was it a dream? Or could we even say it was something of both? We are left with something to think about.

Modern Initiation

In exploring Dorothy's journey we have looked at it as an initiation experience. It was a modern initiation with few of the features of initiation practices of the past. Missing are the usual ideas associated with ancient initiation rituals. Actually, there were no rituals at all. But nonetheless the essence of an initiation was there.

It is of importance that an understanding of the "essence of initiation" be carried on in our culture so that it can be supported in modern times. We may approach it differently than our ancestors but we still need to reap the value of it for our individual growth, as well as our collective well-being. We can look at the events of our own lives as part of an initiation, as we have done with Dorothy's journey.

Dorothy's initiation began when her outer world started giving away—giving away to something new. The mounting pressure of circumstances were showing how Aunt Em and Uncle Henry were reaching the end of what they could give as her guardians. The three farm hands could at best only advise Dorothy to use her brain, heart and courage. With the threat of losing her dear companion Toto, Dorothy did just that, taking initiative and activating her soul capacities. In running away she cut the cord to her outer support system and began an exploration of her inner one. Her initiation began.

Dorothy's new found independence was reflected in her inner realm in the demise of the Wicked Witch of the East and the Mayor of Munchkinland declaring it a day of independence. Empowered with the Witch's magic shoes Dorothy stepped out on a journey full of challenges and trials to test how she would use her power. Would she be a good witch or a bad witch?

From the start, the road proved to be anything but straightforward. To help her, Dorothy gathered up her soul forces of thinking, feeling and will in her companions the Scarecrow, Tin Man and Lion. We see them in a sad state when she first meets them. They are confused thinking, stuck feelings and a will paralyzed with fear. But these capacities were to become her allies in the adventure. This indicates how the spiritual journey is not a matter of bypassing our soul—our thoughts, feelings and will, but rather bringing them along. For Dorothy to complete her journey they had to transform into clear thinking, impassioned feelings and courage of will; or clarity, enthusiasm and determination. As they did, they became the very vehicle that assisted her on her spiritual sojourn.

As Dorothy moved toward her *home goal* she had to work through whatever came before her. Obstacles emerged to oppose her progress. But what they gave her was exactly what she needed at each stage of her journey, and prepared her for what would come in the next. Even when she got off the path and into the poppy field, it was something that needed to happen. It was a breakdown that allowed a breakthrough into her next stage of initiation.

Peril and possible enslavement pursued Dorothy every step of the way. But as she forged forth, her initiation lead to the further activation of her inner resources; and the creative tension of her dualistic nature to her individuality. Along the way she had to face the Wicked Witch of the West and confront the Humbug Wizard. Even their tyrannical and critical ways were something with which Dorothy needed to wrestle. Independence does not come without effort. It is what it took for her to find her power and set herself free.

In facing the Wicked Witch Dorothy tapped more deeply into her own resources. When the Witch melted, it signified the increased empowerment of the self. The transfer of the broom to Dorothy was symbolic of this. The Wizard, when confronted, also was transformed—crediting the others for their accomplishments before he disappeared. Out of these two aspects emerged newly formed powers for Dorothy. Dorothy as the self, assumed her rightful place in the inner domain, inheriting the power of her spiritual parentage.

Dorothy claimed her power, as opposed to giving it away. But not only did she realize her power, she overcome her fear of using it. Furthermore, in a world where the decadent use of power runs rampant, in response to the Good Witch's question, "Are you a good witch or a bad witch?" she proved her ability to use it rightly.

Self-initiation

For the most part, the path of modern initiation is something we go alone. Regarded as a fairy tale, all the characters involved in Dorothy's inner realm were her own parts. Thus the help she received was from within herself. She received diminishing outer support and answered the call to greater self-determination.

The Good Witch instructed Dorothy to follow the Yellow Brick Road. Following the Yellow Brick Road could be considered as following the moment-by-moment guidance of the Higher Self. Nothing compelled Dorothy to follow this path. There were other paths she could have taken. But as she freely followed the guidance given her, she found the way of "self-initiation," the way by which we initiate ourselves, out of ourselves. This is in contrast to the ancient ways of initiation, where a hierophant, priest, or shaman led an initiation ceremony. Dorothy wore no ornate garment, had no candles, no incense, no chanting, nor any of the customary accompaniments of ancient initiations. Not that any of these things necessarily lack value for our personal development. Some may choose to incorporate these and other features into their spiritual lifestyle, and find them beneficial. Ritual has its place. But what is most important is that the *essence of initiation* be understood and encouraged, as it is illustrated archetypally in Dorothy's story. Then, as we experience aspects of initiation found in everyday life and common occurrences, we can work with them rightly to foster our personal spiritual growth. We can take up the task of *self-initiation*.

The young people of today especially need to understand this. Our modern culture is becoming bereft of consciously created outlets for the inherent impulses of initiation. In some ways it is becoming hostile to them. But from another perspective this is perhaps the way it needs to be. As shown by Dorothy, the way of modern initiation is found right in the experience of life itself—not in stepping outside of it. "Being spiritual" is in how we face the challenges that come spontaneously to us, wherever we may be, rather than in contrived ritual. It is how we deal with the conflicts that arise naturally in our associations with others. Initiation comes in the ingenuity and effort we use to work creatively and transformatively for advancement against a tide of distractions and seductions.

The dances with death, violence and use of drugs seen in young people today is, in the majority of cases, more than an attempt to escape the realities of this world. At its root is a sincere attempt to initiate latent capacities. It is an expression of the natural yearning to expand the boundaries of consciousness and embrace the reality of the other world—allowing its life-giving influences to flow into this one. Unknowingly, it is something of a reenactment of initiation practices of the past, lurking in the collective unconscious. But we live in a new age and there are new ways open to us to achieve spiritual experiences similar to the past—and much more.

Initiation and Information

When Dorothy reached the end of her initiation journey she found she could have gone home at anytime. When asked by the Scarecrow, "Why didn't you tell her before?" Glinda responded, "Because she wouldn't have believed me. She had to learn it for herself." Any knowledge we do not acquire for ourselves we will not believe and be able to act on in the long run. Once Dorothy gained the learning she needed, and found the knowledge she was missing, she was able to take herself home—with no more waiting.

We are all in the midst of a new and great *information gathering*. Many of the old ways and old rules have passed. The modern spiritual journey is about finding for ourselves what we need to know to complete our journeys. It is about integrating the information of experience into our beingness. Although overall, the requisite steps are archetypal, the process will be different for every person. That is part of what becoming an individual means. But as each of us gets there, we will all be able to say and mean the same thing as Dorothy, when she said, "There's no place like home."

Initiation and Independence

Dorothy's initiation portrays a journey from *innocence* to *independence*. Before her journey Dorothy was still nested in naivete—untouched by the realities of life. She had a childlike dependency on others, including Toto. But Dorothy's journey has made a difference in her. Now how will it make a difference in her lifestyle?

Dorothy is back on the farm the same as before, but she is not the same as before and so things will be different. She is still made up of the same parts, but each has undergone a transformation and been put together in a new way. As a newly integrated creation she is now greater than the sum of her parts. This will be reflected in her relationship to others.

At the end of the journey Glinda told Dorothy, "You don't need to be helped any longer." Dorothy can now help herself. She has proven herself as an independent being, able to take responsibility for herself. Instead of being dependent on others she can now be dependent on herself. She is capable of independent thought, independent feelings and independent action. She can do for herself what at one time others did for her.

What this translates into is that Dorothy is now independent of Auntie Em and Uncle Henry. It does not mean she has to stay away from them. She simply had to go away to get herself together. She has returned to the same surroundings but inwardly has left the nest. Dorothy has "individuated" or separated out, breaking the ties that would ultimately bind her, including blood-ties. But now she is free to rejoin the whole. She can be her own person wherever she is, with whomever, including her family on the farm.

Dorothy can now be with the same people in a new way. She can be *interdependent* in her relationship to them, side-stepping the trap of *codependency* or undue dependency. By going through the intermediate stage of gaining independence, to establish her own capabilities, she can enjoy an interdependent relationship with others, "interdependent" meaning neither wholly dependent nor wholly independent.

Love is intended to be the bloom of our learning. In this newly found way of relating, the door to a new kind of love is now open. The act of love can be a choice. Love can be a freely given gift. With consciousness Dorothy can give of what she has made of herself, and share it with the rest of the world.

Dorothy's Future

What would the future be for Dorothy? Both the book and film leave it open to speculation. From one perspective one could say Dorothy's journey shows the fulfillment of all human striving—it is archetypally complete and Dorothy's work is finished. But it is more realistic to say she still has more work to do.

For one thing Dorothy's spiritual work will need to be proven in the material world. We can do work on the level of soul and spirit but it eventually has to be established on the physical level—one of the reasons we have physical bodies. In the outer world Dorothy will have opportunities to manifest what she has achieved inwardly and to test the integrity of her integrative work.

When we bring change to our inner world our outer world changes. Our inner work becomes reflected outwardly, experienced as shifts in our perception, and even the actual circumstances surrounding us. If we have taken ownership of our inner dynamics, and worked transformatively with them, we don't need the shadow of them cast so strongly upon the backdrop of human drama. If we have brought the light of consciousness to them, our shadow aspects need not stalk us so darkly—as Miss Gulch initially did with Dorothy. And so one could surmise that the need for Miss Gulch is gone—the dynamic dissolved and the conflict resolved. For some unforeseen reason Miss Gulch will no longer find cause for further action against Dorothy, and Toto will be left alone by her. But as Dorothy carries on down the road of life, she will undoubtedly discover she has more "spiritual blind spots." And so there will be more outer events which will lead to more inner journeys.

Describing the Spiritual Journey

Some readers may still be under the notion that this book is actually about *The Wizard of Oz*. True, this book has gone through *The Wizard of Oz,* but its main theme is really about you and me and the archetypal journey.

Means other than a fairy tale could be used to do the same thing, and in fact have been.

At the same time as we looked at *The Wizard of Oz*, two other languages have been employed to describe the spiritual journey. *Sacred geometry* or the language of symbols, creating the mandala, has been used throughout. Also, the language of modern psychology or *spiritual psychology* has been used. Three languages—the language of a fairy tale, geometry and psychology have been used interchangeably, each describing the same thing, in a different way. Individually as well as collectively they act as a map for the modern spiritual journey.

Using the Map

The mandala on the front cover, now invested with meaning by the content of this book, depicts the road home in a picture. Mandalas have generally been used to guide meditation and to facilitate the development of consciousness. This mandala, if taken as a tool, will be found to have varied uses. To give a simple example, consider how a map is used. A map helps us to get oriented to where we are and indicates where we could go next. This mandala acts in the same way—helping us get oriented to where we are on the Yellow Brick Road and to choose what direction we might pursue.

The mandala helps us to ask questions like—What part of my soul am I in the most—my thinking, my feelings, my will? What part of my soul needs extra attention? What is my relationship to my Witch and Wizard aspects? Do I have more levity than gravity in my life? How is the balance between light and dark, life and death, male and female? Have I invited the help of my Higher Self into the mediation of the dualistic dynamics? How strongly do I include this part in my overall makeup? And what about the Dorothy in me? How is my sense of self? Is it strong? Is it weak? Is it growing? As with any map, the map itself does not take us anywhere. It only makes it clearer where we are and where we may go. It is up to us to get there.

The above is more of an analytical approach to personal exploration. The power of the story can be taken a step further and used in more of an "intuitive" fashion. The characters representing our archetypal parts can be used for actual journeys into ourselves. They can be used in "active imagination." For example, while in an appropriate space you can simply close your eyes and ask the characters to come before your mind's eye, as in a daydream. How does *your* Scarecrow or Tin Man look? What is the setting they are in? What is the mood surrounding them? What is the dynamic between them? Are they close or far apart? Is one in front of the other? What is their relationship to Dorothy, the self? How does she look? Wait for visual, auditory and kinesthetic responses. What do they tell you? This is an introduction to something that, when used properly, can be a powerful tool for personal exploration and development.

Fare Thee Well on the Yellow Brick Road

Ironically, Dorothy was on her way home from school, the formal place of education, when some of her greatest learning began. Life is our greatest teacher if we treat our lifetime as classtime. To help keep this perspective, you might consider some of the following suggestions.

Practice self-reflection. Think about your life. Digest it. Record your journey in a journal. Look at the events in your life as parts of an ongoing initiation.

Develop a closer relationship with your thoughts, feelings and intentions. How else can you think, feel and act for yourself if you are not in touch with your own soul?

Familiarize yourself with the dualities of life. Nature is a library of information about these spiritual principles that are infinitely at work in the manifest realm as well as within ourselves. Observe your own relationship to them.

Invoke your Higher Self. Your connection to your Higher Power gives purpose and direction to your life, leading you along your own personal Yellow Brick Road.

Be artistic. It becomes apparent as the journey progresses that the task of self-development is a highly artistic one. It is the highest art form. What has been laid out conceptually in this book needs to be lived artistically. An artistic sense should be acquired if not already possessed. Being involved in the arts, not simply as a patron but as a participant can contribute greatly to one's development, whether it be through dance, drama, painting, sculpting or one of the many art forms that are available.

Take initiative. Initiative comes from the inside out. Like those baby chicks breaking out of their shells at the beginning of the film, it takes initiative to break through to the other side. We need to shed the shell of naivete that keeps us unaware and unable to participate in the fullness of life.

Make time for personal development. In this age of quick fixes many people are used to instant results with little effort. Even Dorothy was in a hurry to get home. When she went to the Wizard with her request he told her to come back later. Dorothy protested, "Tomorrow? But I want to go home now!" But initiation involves growth processes —it takes time, so give it time.

On the other hand, time is not unlimited. There is a certain urgency for humanity to develop the consciousness needed to meet the new and diverse challenges arising on the planet. As they neared the Emerald City, Dorothy and her soul parts said to each other, "Well come on then. What are you waiting for?" "Hurry! Hurry!" "You can't rest now—we're nearly there."

About the author

The author considers himself best termed "a philosopher," (*philo sophia*)—a lover of knowledge and wisdom. From an early age he has been intrigued with the mysteries of life. His formal education has taken him through various trainings but for the most part is self-taught. His studies include the areas of spirituality, psychology, education and the arts. He sees his work as the synthesizing of these different fields in the new paradigm.

About the art and artist

The diagrams evolved on their own during the development of the material for this book, culminating in the cover art. Design and implementation was by artist Dave Varing of Boulder, Colorado with Jesse Stewart.

Direct any correspondence for the author to:
238 Davenport Road
Box 295
Toronto, Ontario
M5R 1J6 Canada
Email: jesse_s@netcom.ca